Life Coaching

Life Coaching

Connecting you to your inner wisdom

Gina Harris

To Stephen

Wishing you always
a 'Perfect Present'
(& a fantastic future..!) *Gina*

Kingsham Press

First published 2002
by Kingsham Press

Oldbury Complex
Marsh Lane
Easthampnett
Chichester, West Sussex
PO18 OJW
United Kingdom

© 2002 Gina Harris

Typeset in AGaramond

Printed and bound by
MPG Books
Bodmin
Cornwall
United Kingdom

ISBN: 1-904235-05-0

British Library Cataloguing in Publication Data
A catalogue record of this book is available from the British Library

Harris, Gina

Acknowledgements

I would like to thank Anand Kumar of Kingsham Press for commissioning me to write this book. It has been an absorbing and instructive process.

Many thanks are also due to all the coaches who have contributed to this book with ideas, case studies and quotes. They include Aboodi Shaby, Bill Ford, Christian Worth, Christina Toft, Christine Baines, Dianna Keel, Dominique Charles, Elizabeth Rowlands, Ginny Baillie, Janice Morris, Jilly Shaul, Mark Forster, Mike Duckett, Rachel Spooncer, Resli Costabell, Sarah Litvinoff, Suzanne Looms and Teresa Marshall.

Several of the case studies included in this book have been adapted from those which originally appeared in the 'Dear Coach' column of *The Times* Saturday Magazine. They were written by Sarah Litvinoff and Elizabeth Rowlands.

The 'Stories' used throughout the text have been adapted from *The Song of the Bird* by the late Anthony de Mello. I wish I could have told him how much I have benefited from his wise and challenging writings.

About the author

Gina Harris is a highly-experienced developer of people. She has been a self-employed trainer and facilitator for ten years and was one of the first licensed trainers for Springboard, the international women's development programme. She is co-author, with Liza Edwards, of *Springing Forward*, an essential handbook for women who want to make the most of their lives.

Gina runs her own successful life coaching business – Access Coaching – and can be contacted via her website: **www.accesscoaching.co.uk**, by email: **enquiries@accesscoaching.co.uk** or by phone on +44 (0) 1335 350540.

"Sonya sat next to me on the long flight from the USA to Switzerland. I was on my way to attend the conference in Grindelwald. She was on her way home to celebrate her 85th birthday.

I asked her what she was most excited about. She said, "I'm celebrating that I don't care so much any more. I work as a volunteer at a hospital because I want to work, not because I need the money. I've just graduated from a computer training class so my mind is still being challenged. I spend time with the people I enjoy and don't waste my energy on politics. Most importantly, after all these years, I am now comfortable with who I am, and I am connected to my inner wisdom."

I smiled. She asked what I did and I explained Life Coaching.

Her reply was, "Ah, coaching is too harsh a word for what you do. You connect people to their inner wisdom *before* they are 85 years old."

From the Opening Address by DJ Mitsch,
President of the International Coaching Federation,
at the ICF European Coaching Conference, May 2001

Dedicated to all my clients – my partners in the rewarding business of discovering a fuller and more satisfying life.

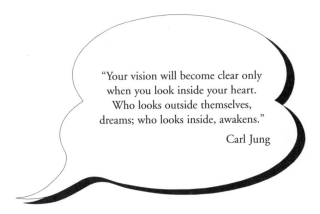

"Your vision will become clear only
when you look inside your heart.
Who looks outside themselves,
dreams; who looks inside, awakens."

Carl Jung

Contents

Welcome

The chief impulse for writing this book was impatience. I was rapidly tiring of people exclaiming, "You're a life coach? What on earth's that?" Their ignorance is excusable. Life coaching is a fairly recent phenomenon in the UK, although it has been around considerably longer in the USA. Beside the need to explain exactly what it is, I also have the desire to spread the word about its value and effectiveness. Once I had discovered this 'better mousetrap', I knew I could not expect people to beat a path to my door – I must wave the mousetrap aloft and shout about its glories. My impatience will turn to delight when the question I hear asked most often about life coaching is not 'What is it?' but 'So who's your coach?'

My own discovery of life coaching is an interesting example of what is now called 'synchronicity'. After several years of involvement in the field of self-development, mainly as a licensed trainer for Springboard, the international women's development programme, I became aware of a gap in the support available to people who took such development seriously and who wanted to continue exploring their potential in a regular, focused and motivating way. I actually wrote down my idea of what I thought was needed – I still have the scribbled notes. Unknown to me, what I had actually written was an accurate description of life coaching. Shortly afterwards, when giving a talk about Springboard, I met Chris Taylor who was to become a much valued mentor and friend. At one of our regular meetings, she gave me some information about Coach University and the light flashed on. So this was what I'd been visualising! I signed up for coach training that very same day.

This book is just one person's experience and understanding of life coaching – mine. There are other coaches more skilled, more knowledgeable and more qualified to do this than I am. When I revealed these doubts to my friends, they all sighed in exasperation and said, "But they aren't writing this book – you are." If I use the term 'we' to convey opinions other than just my own, I would like you to remember the quote from Simone Weil: "*Every sentence that begins with 'we' is a lie.*"

My book will have done its job if it simply tells you enough about life coaching for you to want to know more. It will have succeeded if it encourages you to find yourself a coach and discover the life you really want to live. If it also inspires you to take on the coaching mindset in all your interactions with other human beings, that will be one more person transforming our world for the better.

Notes

You will find many quotations in this book. There are several reasons for this. Firstly, as my friends will tell you, I devour books for my learning and inspiration and I don't see the point of trying to put something in my own words when someone else has said it much better. Secondly, I want to show how widespread and how all-encompassing many of the ideas expressed here have become, from the business world to esoteric fields of spirituality, from well-respected gurus to hands-on practitioners. Thirdly, just a taste of a book I've found instructive and inspiring may persuade you to read the original and find a new source of knowledge and revelation. And lastly, there is something delightfully compact and memorable about a good quotation. The book will be worthwhile if you find just one quote that is so meaningful to you that it changes your life.

Throughout the book, when writing in general terms, I use 'he' for the client and 'she' for the coach for two reasons: firstly, because it provides a useful short-hand method of distinguishing between the two, and secondly, because it celebrates the fact that coaching is a profession where there are as many female practitioners as male.

ONE

What is life coaching?

Listen to these voices:

Ian: I work in the family pottery business, like my father and my grandfather did. It was taken for granted that this was my career, ready mapped out for me. It's not bad but it's not what I really want to do for the rest of my life. Can't see how to get out of it though, without causing a lot of grief in the family.

Tamsin: I'd expected to be married with a couple of kids by the time I was thirty, but it hasn't happened. Not much I can do about it. Join a dating agency perhaps. Can't see me doing that. Just have to resign myself to being an old maid.

Barry: In one way, I feel great because I've just been promoted into my dream job. I know I can do it well but there's some aspects where I'm completely at sea. I can't tell anyone; don't want it to look as if I can't cope. I'll just have to muddle through and hope I don't make any major cock-ups!

Jody: I'd love to set up my own business and I've got a really great idea for this. But it's risky – I'm in a well-paid job, and I've got some large debts to pay off. Oh well, just another pipe dream I suppose....

Peter: I've been working in the Middle East – made quite a bit of money which I've invested well. I'm engaged to a wonderful girl so every thing's going well but I need to choose my next job wisely and I really want us to have a fantastic relationship in our marriage. This will be the second time for me and I don't want to make the same mistakes again.

Steve: My life's a real mess. I work too hard at a job I hate, my girlfriend's just dumped me because she says I'm never there for her, and now the sale on my flat's fallen through. How do I survive all this?

So which of these people would benefit from investing in a life coach? The answer, of course, is all of them. As the steady stream of books, articles and programmes in the media demonstrate, life coaching is a rapidly growing profession. But what exactly is it?

The origins

Coaching has existed since people started talking and listening to each other and has throughout history been a means of motivating and encouraging. What we are witnessing here is the relatively new form of coaching which has been formalised under the title 'life coaching'.

Life coaching in its present form began in the 1980s in the USA. Thomas J Leonard, then a financial adviser in Seattle, discovered as he worked that many of his clients needed more than the basic financial planning he was offering. They asked his advice on many issues regarding their own career ambitions and their life planning. Leonard used the word 'coaching' for this process which became increasingly popular, covering as it did far more than finances. In 1982, Leonard started his own coaching practice and is credited with first using the term 'coaching' in a non-sporting context. He organised what he had learned about coaching into a formal structure of knowledge and techniques. In 1992 Leonard set up Coach University (CoachU), now the largest coach training organisation in the world, to allow others to benefit from his work. By 1996, about 2,000 people were full-time life coaches. The number of people entering the profession has doubled each year in the last three years and there are an estimated 10,000 part-time and full-time coaches worldwide. CoachU estimates that 250,000 people have been coached in the last ten years.

Sporting comparisons

The first image usually brought to mind by the word 'coach' is an enthusiastic and sometimes bullying figure haranguing a football team or a budding athlete. Probably the nearest sporting relation to a life coach is a personal trainer. You pay someone to give you one-to-one attention, to help you set goals and work out a strategy to reach them. The trainer then keeps you committed and dismisses any excuses for avoiding the work required to get your body into the shape you want it to be. A life coach follows a similar process to help you get your life into the shape you want it to be. Champions, at the peak of their sport, are the ones who seem least likely to need a coach, yet often they attribute much of their success to their coach. It's ironic that where life coaching is concerned, the reaction very often is, "There's nothing wrong with you – you don't need a coach!"

No self-respecting athlete or football team would dream of trying to succeed without the regular help and encouragement of a coach. Both sporting and life coaches have certain features in common:

- The only goal of the coach is to bring out the best in the client and to ensure that at all times, the client is performing at his peak.
- The skills and strategies of teamwork may well be encouraged as part of the client's path to success.
- Going for the goal, or goals, will be one of the main purposes of the coach's sessions.
- No serious sportsman or woman would dream of attempting to get to the top completely on their own.
- Similarly, a person who wants to succeed in life – whatever that means to each individual – understands the vital role a coach can play.

Where sports and life coaching differ

The sporting coach is, or has been, an expert in the game. The life coach is an expert primarily in the job of coaching, though she may also have specialist knowledge in the client's profession.

Life coaching is not competitive or win/lose based; the client is competing only against himself and improving performance only for his own satisfaction.

Want to buy a bike?

There are several kinds of professionals who offer services very similar to coaching and it's important to differentiate coaching clearly from these. Many coaches explain exactly what they do by using the analogy of choosing and buying your first bicycle.

A **counsellor** will talk to you about what's stopping you just going out and buying a bike. She will raise your awareness of the blocks that you have and ask what your fears are. She will discuss with you all the issues involved in the purchase of a bicycle – the make, the model, the colour. After counselling, you'll feel able to go and buy your bike unaided and with confidence.

Counsellors help people to overcome difficulties in their lives and often specialise in a particular area or issue, so there are counsellors who deal specifically in bereavement, relationships, infertility, post-traumatic stress and so on. The popular image of a counsellor is someone gentle and caring, prepared to spend as long as it takes to help the client to function effectively again. This is a somewhat different approach from the straight-talking directness of coaching. A coach will tell you the truth from the very first session onwards. She will say what she sees and not wait for you to discover it for yourself. Coaching is aimed at those who are mentally healthy.

A **therapist** will also be likely to discuss the blocks regarding your purchase of a bike, but will go on to ask how this particular problem affects the rest of your life. Your difficulties in buying a bike will be the catalyst for exploring many other issues with you and looking at the wider picture of your life as a whole.

Therapy helps patients confront and deal with their past in order to cope better in the future. The coach, however, is not looking for the roots of behaviour but at the results. She will not ask 'Why do you behave like this?' but rather 'How can you begin to behave differently?' Coaching doesn't work on 'issues', dig into the client's past, or deal with understanding human behaviour. The coach's main concern is not with explanations or causes, though these may figure briefly from time to time. The amount of time allowed for negative talk is severely restricted.

What the coach is interested in is the present, the habits, attitudes and behaviour that the client can amend if he so wishes and the future, the new skills and attitudes needed to achieve the goals he sets himself.

During the sessions, a trained coach is likely to become aware if a client is in need of psychological care. The client may be consistently refusing to address a specific area of his life, avoiding dealing with a particular subject, or giving vent to abnormally strong emotions. The coach may then suggest that he seeks help from a therapist before continuing with the coaching.

A **consultant** will research the different types of bicycle available and put together a report comparing the different makes, styles and models. He may offer advice on which would suit you best and even give you instructions on how to ride it.

A consultant is usually an expert on some area of business or knowledge – that is why he or she is being consulted. A coach may have no specific expertise (though many coaches do) but is simply an expert at being a coach. Both consultants and coaches share information and expertise with the client but the coach asks for, and expects, personal growth and change.

> "It is . . . so hard for experts to withhold their expertise sufficiently to coach well."
>
> John Whitmore

A **mentor** tells you about his experience of bike riding, the problems he had and how he overcame them. He gives advice about mending punctures, how to brake safely and how to ride sensibly through heavy traffic. He may also introduce you to some expert cyclists and recommend a good bicycle repair shop.

A mentor is usually someone older and more experienced with specific knowledge and skills to pass on. As an expert in a particular field or company, a mentor knows the job and can guide someone less experienced or younger. The emphasis in mentoring is likely to be on teaching what the mentor knows, whereas in coaching it is on discovering what the client knows.

> "An independent coach can reflect ideas, evoke solutions and support their implementation in a way that few insiders could ever do."
>
> John Whitmore

One problem with mentoring in the workplace is that the mentor has his own job to do – which of course he must put first – and so is not likely to be regularly available for the necessary sessions. The coach's whole job is to coach and to put your needs as her priority.

A **parent** will choose your bike and buy it for you. He may insist on putting stabilisers on it to start with and take them off only when he thinks you will be safe without them. He will hold the back of the saddle as you learn to ride properly and take away his supporting hand when you're not looking. He will decide when and where you may ride your bike and may punish you if you disobey the rules.

A parent empowers the child, provides unconditional love and support, feels at least partly responsible for the end result and has a vested interest in the outcome. A coach is not responsible for the end result, can ask for more and is not cautious or protective but treats the client as an adult. In spite of some popularly-held beliefs to the contrary, a coach is not a 'professional nag'.

> "In professional coaching, accountability does not include blame, scolding, punishment or judgment."
>
> Laura Whitworth et al

A **friend** may appear really enthusiastic about your plans to take up cycling. She'll go with you to the shop, show some interest at first before getting bored, asking how long you'll be and saying she'll see you later in the coffee shop. She'll admire your purchase and offer to come and help you when you go for your first ride. She may indeed even be there to pick you up when you fall off. But this will also be the point at which she decides that cycling is not such a good idea and will persuade you to put the bike in the shed and go to the cinema instead.

Friends are vital, but they are not professional coaches and find it hard to be completely objective. If they want to remain your friends, there will be many times when telling you the unpleasant truth is not an option. When you're successful, your friends are not always utterly delighted, unlike your coach. Some of your friends may have a vested interest in keeping you the way you are and feel threatened by any changes you may choose to make, especially if the change affects them directly. Competitive friends particularly may feel alienated or jealous. While having your well-being and success at the heart of her relationship with you, your coach is not, and will not try to be, your friend. She needs to expect and demand far more from you than a friend ever would.

A **coach** listens to you talk about your desire to try cycling. She will ask questions to discover exactly what sort of cycling you want to do and whether you know what kind of bicycle you'd like. She may ask you to do a bit of research on bikes and bike shops and ask you to name the exact day that you'll buy your bike. She'll help you get on, run along beside you while you learn to ride it and check from time to time that you're really enjoying it. She won't stop you falling off, but she'll be there to make sure you've learned why the accident happened and how you can prevent it happening again. Together, you'll talk about what the experience of cycling is like for you and whether you want to become an expert cyclist, just cycle for pleasure, or get rid of the bike now you've tried it because it's not as exciting as you thought. Whatever you decide, your coach will be there to listen, question and support you.

So life coaching is:

➤ **An extraordinarily focused method of personal development**
There's just you and your coach. During the formal sessions, the client gets the full and undivided attention of the coach.

➤ **A supportive relationship of equals**
The foundation of the coaching partnership is that it is one of equals. The coach does not talk down to or impose her own views on the client. The coach is an expert at coaching. The client is an expert on himself and his own life. Coaching only works properly if this equality is understood at the beginning and reinforced throughout the coaching relationship.

➤ **A relationship of accountability**
Being equal also means that responsibility is also equally divided. The main responsibility of the coach is to bring out the best in the client. For the client, the main responsibility is to take charge of his own life and to do whatever has been agreed between him and his coach. The client is held accountable for his own results. The coach is detached from the client's results in order to keep her own objectivity and professionalism.

➤ **A way of making changes, internally and externally**

The initial impulse for hiring a coach is to make changes. These may not necessarily be external – they may be changes in attitude, in thinking, in assumptions. Life coaching, by definition, addresses the whole of life. Nothing is 'off limits' unless the client decides it should be so and even then, the coach may warn that the client who puts a barrier around certain subjects will not get full value from the coaching sessions, or succeed in making the kind of changes he wants to make.

➤ **A body of knowledge relating to the development of human potential**

As Thomas J Leonard explains in his book 'The Portable Coach':

> "Coaching has now evolved into an integrated success technology. It's more than a couple of principles and techniques. It's a well-woven fabric of hundreds of specialised skills, principles, concepts, practices and nuggets of wisdom."

Life coaching has its critics, mainly in those fields most closely associated with it – psychiatry, psychotherapy, counselling. Life coaches are not required to get clinical training and, at the time of writing, not licensed or accredited by law, though progress towards this is currently being made. Coaches do not claim to be mental health care professionals. They are not dealing with problems but with challenges, dilemmas and opportunities. Coach training is an amalgam of techniques from a whole range of professions, together with some peculiarly its own. There are few hard and fast rules about the process of coaching because the coach responds to the client's agenda. The heart of coaching is the client's goals, strategies and solutions, not the coach's.

Coaches are occasionally accused of dabbling in areas that they don't understand and aren't qualified to deal with. But a properly trained coach will know when the client needs something other than coaching and will point the client towards the appropriate expert. If this referral would not have been made but for the coaching, then coaches are manifestly doing more good than harm.

> "One of the reasons why coaching is expanding so rapidly as a profession is that people are well intentioned. They know what they need to do, know what they want, at least in general terms. They say they'll do this or that with genuine goodwill but then life gets in the way."

Laura Whitworth et al

For the vast majority of people, the big issues of life are rarely, if ever, given the time and attention they deserve. For those individuals who decide to take action, a life coach acts as a bridge, spanning the gulf between where they are now and where they want to be. A committed person asking "How do I get started on making my life how I want it to be?" is music to a life coach's ears.

TWO

Why do we need it?

"Everything is pretty much up for grabs right now. There are many world views in contention. There is much transition. There's a sense of disorientation. There is a deconstruction, or tearing down of many long-established principles...."

Richard Tarnas

Our society isn't functioning as well as it might and we are seeing rapid changes in a number of areas. There is an overriding feeling of living through a transitional period. For better or worse, many of the supports and certainties that previously helped people to live in a structured way are no longer firmly in place. These changes have resulted in a need for people generally to make far more, and far deeper, decisions with less clear guidance than in the generations before.

All change in the family

If you delve back into your family history, you'll probably find that your great-grandparents, possibly even your grandparents, lived very settled, traditional lives, the pattern for which was provided by the community in which they lived. They and their neighbours would have had very clear ideas about what was right and wrong, about taking care of each other and about what their duties and responsibilities were. Not a lot would have been heard about 'human rights' or 'individual expression'. Anyone who stepped outside the accepted boundaries – the unmarried woman who gave birth to a child or a young man who refused to go into his father's business – were considered to be 'wrong' and were treated accordingly. We can't, and probably don't want, to live as our predecessors lived but that doesn't mean we don't regret some of what we've lost.

The waning stability of marriage is an obvious case in point. It seems that everywhere divorce rates are rising. This is not necessarily a 'bad thing' if some of the reasons for this rise are the decline in the disapproval that previously locked people into a lifetime of unhappiness, and the improved financial situation of many women who used to be wholly dependent on their husbands.

In *Emotional Intelligence*, Daniel Goleman writes:

> "….if social pressures are no longer the glue that holds a marriage together, then the emotional forces between wife and husband are that much more crucial if their union is to survive."

How are these emotional forces to be harnessed and used for enhancement of the marriage rather than its destruction? There is the possibility that this epidemic of divorce is a transition into a new model of marriage, more of an equal partnership and less of a superior obeyed by an inferior. The divorce rates are often seen as a sign of society's disintegration but could equally be the necessary passage towards a different view of marriage.

As the traditional household of two parents, one male, one female, living with their birth children declines speedily, it also heralds a more inclusive view of what constitutes a family – divorced people who have remarried and now live with their children from previous marriages, step children and children born since the remarriage. Parenthood is in the melting pot. Some families still function with a dictatorial father and a submissive mother along traditional Victorian lines; others work more like a miniature democracy with all members being considered equal and even the very young ones being consulted on family issues.

There are also the dilemmas faced by working mothers, by fathers trapped in the long hours culture at work, by grandparents expecting a quiet retirement but being pressured into grandchild care by lack of crèches or nursery school places. People are living longer than ever before and therefore married couples are facing the prospect of living with someone not for twenty or thirty years but possibly fifty or sixty, when often each has grown in a different direction and with diverse interests.

For many of us, scenarios like these are not just academic but in need of urgent solutions because we're living with them every day. Who can we talk to who will listen to our problems, in confidence and without forcing their own agenda on us? How do we compensate for the lack of a close-knit community and how do we make the most of the general encouragement towards self-expression? Such challenging dilemmas are the stuff of which life coaching is made, as the following case shows.

Deanna

In her early fifties, with two grown-up sons, Deanna was looking forward to moving from part-time to full-time work and promotion as a social worker specialising in children with Attention Deficit Disorder (ADD). However, she realised that her older husband, approaching retirement, was equally anticipating their having more time together and taking things easier. Deanna told her coach, "I don't know what to do – he's so full of plans for the two of us in his retirement. But I feel it's my turn to get somewhere with my career, now the boys have left home. I'm certainly not ready to put my feet up yet."

Her coach helped Deanna to work out a strategy that would enable both partners to live the lives they really wanted. It became clear to Deanna she had enough specialist knowledge to set herself up as an independent therapist, working from home. It was an exciting venture which gave Deanna all the challenge she was seeking. But it also meant that her husband saw much more of her, was able to help out with setting up her office and some of the administration. In return, Deanna set herself strong boundaries around when she was working and when she wasn't and set aside regular days for the two of them to spend time together – days which her husband greatly enjoyed planning.

All change in church

- Who am I?
- What is my place in the world?
- What am I here for?
- What is the purpose of life?

> "Most of us today have moved away from the religious structures that once supplied answers to these questions, but the questions themselves have not gone away."
>
> John R O'Neil

Statistics on attendance at churches in this country indicate that the numbers of people actively signing up to membership of a formal religion are falling. But this does not necessarily indicate a decline in the thirst for spirituality – a very important distinction.

A story

The master was asked, "What is spirituality?"

He said, "Spirituality is that which succeeds in bringing one to inner transformation."

"But if I apply the traditional methods handed down by the masters, is that not spirituality?"

"It is not spirituality if it does not perform its function for you. A blanket is no longer a blanket if it does not keep you warm."

"So spirituality does change?"

"People change and needs change. So what was spirituality once is spirituality no more. What generally goes under the name of spirituality is merely the record of past methods."

Martin Seligman sums up the situation when he writes of:

> "...the ascendancy of individualism and a waning of larger beliefs in religion, and in support from the community and extended family. That means a loss of resources that can buffer you against setbacks and failures."

There is no point in attempting to turn the clock back. Once people have decided to throw away the security blanket of traditional religion, many explore and discover a new kind of spirituality, one that is appropriate and meaningful to them in today's world. One of the more profound roles for the life coach is to assist people in their exploration of spirituality, in a way that feeds the mind and nourishes the soul, avoiding the danger of becoming a 'straw in the wind' – believing in anything rather than nothing.

All change for women

The western world has been dominated for many centuries by masculine power but the last century has seen huge changes in the status of women. For the majority of women today, the traditional role of lifelong, full-time dependent housewife and/or mother is not the ideal or indeed, for many, an option. The figures regarding the financial position of women in households today show a very different story from male breadwinner and female home-maker. Women, struggling to do it all and often blaming themselves because they can't, are becoming exhausted and confused. There have been few initiatives politically to acknowledge or support them in their new roles.

> "Housewife, New Woman, Superwoman, Homemaker, Career Woman – throughout the twentieth century women have been defining and redefining what it means to be a woman."
>
> Harriet Harman

In fact it's mostly men, particularly those in the media, who have been doing the defining and the redefining. But women, willingly or unwillingly, take all these labels on board and find that they now have an increasing number of new and important decisions to make about the sort of life they want to lead. Even as they become more aware of these decisions, women have less and less time in which to think about them. The effects of all these changes on women today provide a rich source of material for female clients and their coaches to work on.

Caroline

As a freelance trainer working from home, divorced and with two small children, Caroline felt her life was out of control. She seemed to stagger from crisis to crisis, trying to juggle the demands of her work, her family and her home. "I'm just so tired most of the time," she told her coach, "and that makes me ratty with the children, which isn't fair on them. The house looks a complete mess and I never seem to have time for myself. Where am I going wrong?"

Her coach helped Caroline to recognise the huge demands she was making on herself and to give herself some credit for what she had already achieved. Then together they worked out a variety of ways in which Caroline could organise her life better and prioritise things differently. She found she could afford to get some help in the house and let go of the belief that she had to do everything herself. She planned weekly menus and ordered groceries once a week over the internet. She was more assertive with the companies that employed her and put her fees up. She tidied the house one room at a time, being ruthless with the clutter. In her diary, she blocked out time with the children and for yoga classes for herself – time which was inviolable. After several months of coaching, Caroline had achieved a much better balance in her life and was able to reduce her coaching sessions to one a month, just to check she was staying relaxed and happy.

All change for men

 *A story*

He was a difficult man. He thought differently and acted differently from the rest of us. He questioned everything. Was he a rebel or a prophet or a psychopath or a hero? "Who can tell the difference?" we said. "And who cares, anyway?" So we *socialized* him. We taught him to be sensitive to public opinion and to the feelings of others. We got him to conform. He was comfortable to live with now. *Well adjusted.* We had made him manageable and docile. We congratulated him on having achieved self-conquest. He began to congratulate himself too. He did not see that it was we who had conquered him.

The changing fortunes of women have meant associated changes in society's attitudes to men and masculinity. The backlash for men is that being male is often now seen as problematic rather than so acceptable as not to require comment.

> "...the incidence of male suicide has increased by 70 per cent in the last dozen years. The very processes which offer men the prospect of some new kinds of freedom have brought others nothing but disintegration and despair."
>
> Dave Hill

The response of some men to the rise of feminism has been to dig in their heels and blame all the ills of society on women's demands for change. This has resulted in what the media love to call 'The War of the Sexes', in spite of the assertion by the majority of both men and women that what is desirable is an equal partnership, not warfare. This equality is made hard to achieve owing to:

> "...the unwillingness or inability of men to adapt or to behave in a well-balanced way. Prised out of their easy chairs in front of the fire, they are unable to get comfortable elsewhere."
>
> Dave Hill

David

When David first spoke to his coach, he said ruefully, "I know exactly how you'll diagnose my problem – it's called 'the male menopause'! I'm fed up with my job and feel I haven't fulfilled my potential, especially when I see all these young things making a million before they're twenty-five. I'd love to do something really adventurous and outrageous, but I've got a family to support and a mortgage to pay. I'm a hopeless case, aren't I?" When his coach had stopped laughing, she asked David a bit about his childhood, what he'd enjoyed doing and what he'd always dreamt of doing when he was 'grown up'.

Digging out his forgotten longings and talking to his wife more about how he felt gave David a new impetus to change his outlook on life and to realise that there were different kinds of 'success'. He began to take more pleasure in his current existence, but also started to plan how he could build in more of the things that would thrill him. "Is there any reason why you shouldn't have a motorbike instead of a car? " asked his coach. "If your wife's car can be used for the family, why not trade yours in for the Harley Davidson you've always wanted? There's such a thing as being too responsible, you know!"

Just this one change was a catalyst for David. Instead of dreading the journey to work, he looked forward to it. He and his coach then began to look at other things he could do to get more of what he really wanted without damaging the security of his family. He has now negotiated a long leave from his job to join an overland trip through Africa. His wife is happy to give him the freedom he needs in return for promises that when she reaches that stage of her life, he'll be equally understanding!

"Women seem to be better trained at friendship from an early age; they know more about how to use friends as advisers and confidants. Perhaps the men's movement will help to make men more aware of their need for friendly coaching and their obligation to provide it for others."

John R O'Neil

For both men and women, the end of the last and the beginning of the present century is a time of transition. Discovering exactly what kind of a man or woman you want to be, and taking steps to become it, is a prime way of making the most of a life coach.

Changes in sexual equality

"Simply by refusing to be invisible, gays have taken issue with the fundamentals of 'official' manhood, a version of masculinity which has frequently been promoted at their direct expense but which has cruelly damaged other men too."

Dave Hill

The rise in the visibility and acceptability of homosexuality brings new freedoms and new challenges. Many gay people have less reason to fear exposure than in previous generations but that doesn't mean there is a clear path for them to walk. Confusion, prejudice and harassment still abound. The question for many in this position is whether to 'come out' and, if so, to whom, when and how? People need a safe environment in which to explore the consequences of possible courses of action and build up the resources needed to deal with the aftermath. A life coach is an invaluable companion to have on such a journey.

Eric

Although living happily with his same-sex partner, Eric, an architect in his mid-twenties, had always concealed from his family the fact that he was gay. Whenever his parents came to stay, he gave them the impression that John was just a friend and flat-mate, and he had never invited John back to the family home in the country. Eric knew his integrity was being compromised and believed he now had the courage to tell the truth. He decided to employ a life coach to support him through the process of 'coming out' to his family.

Working out exactly what he wanted to say, how and when to say it, and how he would cope with the fall-out were the main subjects of Eric's coaching sessions, which included some practical role plays. Although the whole experience was uncomfortable for Eric, the results were much better than he had expected. His family were surprised and not a little shocked, but with time, they accepted the situation and made John welcome in their home. "I wish I'd done this much sooner," Eric told his coach, "but I probably wouldn't have done it at all without your help."

Changes in the environment

"…we are using up the world the way a drunk uses up his body – heading for a premature death."

Robert Aitken

Another area of relatively new decision-making pitfalls is that of the environment. Issues around the future of our planet are discussed with an urgency never felt before. People of conscience want to ensure that they are doing as much as they can to preserve life and diminish pollution. Again, for the individual there are lifestyle options to be considered and decisions to be made about downsizing, recycling, consumerism, our treatment of animals, use of unsustainable fuels, genetic engineering – the list is endless. For many thoughtful individuals, these are priority issues. Using a life coach can be a structured way of confronting these dilemmas and making informed choices.

The changing workplace

What I wouldn't give for a nine to five.
Biscuits in the right hand drawer,
teabreaks, and typists to mentally undress.
The same faces. Somewhere
to hang your hat and shake your umbrella.
Cosy. Everything in its place.
Upgraded every few years. Hobbies.
Glass of beer at lunchtime
Pension to look forward to. . .

An extract from *Cosy Biscuit* by Roger McGough

The world of work used to be clear-cut and dependable. You got a good education, ideally went to university, or if not, entered an apprenticeship or some other form of on-the-job training. You then moved gradually up the ladder, stopping at the point at which you or your employer felt was right for you, and remained in that position until the statutory retirement age. Of course there were many variations on this theme but certain principles were taken as read:

- You were lucky to have a job
- You stayed in your job as long as you could
- Your were not dismissed for anything less than a gross misdemeanour, unless you were laid off because of a recession
- You were never paid as much as you thought you were worth

- You judged your success and the success of others by the positions you held at work

The workplace offered stability, order and a reasonably assured livelihood, if you didn't blot your copybook. What it wasn't expected to offer were fulfilling or even pleasurable experiences – these were what happened outside work, if at all. Work equalled money and status. Nothing much else was expected of it. Having a job gave huge numbers of people a reason to get up in the morning but very few had the motivation to leap out of bed with the anticipation of an interesting and challenging day ahead. Many workers were square pegs in round holes but they were not expected to complain or even to notice this uncomfortable fit. People simply did not expect to get work that satisfied or fulfilled them.

> "But though the job world has provided continuity, order, and a sense of identity, it has also made many people miserable. Not only were many of us pigeonholed – and in the wrong slots – many of us find repetitive, work-within-the-lines temperamentally difficult."
>
> William Bridges

For many workers, not a lot has changed. But for an increasing number, especially the burgeoning number of young graduates, things are very different today. The choice of jobs on offer, the variety of courses and methods by which to become skilled and qualified, the expectations that moving between different jobs and different companies is not merely acceptable but sought for are all relatively new developments. Most revolutionary of all is the realisation that your working life is something to be planned, created and moulded by you. You are responsible for choosing the work you do and even the ways, times and places in which you do it.

Melanie

"I'm in my late thirties and I work as a manager in a construction firm. I enjoy the work but I don't seem to be getting anywhere. I think the trouble is that I don't have any specialist skills – I'm not an engineer, an accountant or an IT whiz. All I've got are good secretarial and organising skills." By talking to her coach, Melanie began to realise that management itself was a very valuable and not easily obtainable set of competencies, but because she didn't recognise what she had to offer, neither did anyone else in the company. She saw that if she wanted promotion, she would have to demonstrate to the senior management what a lot she had to contribute.

Her coach helped her to work out a strategy for pinpointing an area in the business which needed attention and in which she could shine. Melanie had often worried about how the company were losing staff because of the general inadequacy of training and development for them. She was able to put together a report which showed without a doubt how costly this was proving to be and also to suggest that she take on the task of setting up an effective training department. This proved to be a winning move and before too long, Melanie was not only working for some qualifications which the company agreed to pay for but she was running her own department, and eventually had a place on the board as well.

"We hunger for clear guidance on how to find work that satisfies our heart and still pays the bills."

Claude Whitmyer

Such guidance comes chiefly from within but a coach can help uncover it and put it to its best use.

The new technology

This is supposed to save us effort but in the short term, it often brings us new problems and frustrations. Many of us are not trained or prepared for the multiple technological appliances we are expected to use. The line between 'working' and 'not working' is becoming increasingly blurred. Pagers, mobile phones, voicemail, email – the common principle seems to be that if people can be instantly contacted, then they should be, however unimportant or non-urgent the message. The buzz phrase '24/7' means constant, round-the-clock availability, which is provided and therefore expected. The majority of us are now so inured to this state of being that few of us question why it needs to be so and whether it's in our best interests. We fear that, if we aren't constantly in touch with our work, it will not be long before our work decides it can manage without us. In many areas of work, people feel they are clinging to their jobs by their fingertips and being non-contactable is paramount to being disposable and therefore sacked.

Techno-stress is a common factor, at home and at work. The capacity of the devices on offer never stabilises. There's always a higher specification, a new upgrade, a faster modem, a better ISP. Few of us are given adequate knowledge or training in the technology on offer. If you work from home without technical support, you face the dreaded obstacle course known as 'ringing the helpline' – the decisions regarding button-pushing, the lack of a real human presence, not to mention the background panic of knowing that as you wait, listening yet again to a tinny rendition of Vivaldi's Four Seasons, the cost is mounting inexorably by a pound a minute.

The opportunity of working from home, either as an employee or in one's own business, is an ambivalent aspect of the new technology. The problems then arise of 'Which is work space and which is home?' 'When am I working and when am I not?' If your workspace is also your bedroom, you have the dubious pleasure of being able to sit up in bed, sipping your morning tea while gazing at your filing cabinet and overloaded desk – hardly a relaxing start to another day's work. Yet the demand for part-time and home-working is increasing in many sectors of the workplace.

So we have a love/hate relationship with the amazing inventions of the twenty-first century. We moan and complain about never being off duty and receiving far more emails than we can possibly deal with. But we love the way all this proves how important we are and how much we're needed. For some of us, it's almost the only indication of our value to others, and consequently, to ourselves. It may seem perverse to complain about the effect these scientific advances are having on our lives but the stresses they cause are undeniable and need to be addressed.

The question of leadership

"The chaos we're experiencing now is just a symptom that the forms that we have been operating under have outlived their usefulness."

Marilyn Ferguson

In general, our leaders continue to behave as if the future were going to be just a different version of the past. It hardly ever is, and it is less likely to be so now than ever before. Most leaders in traditional positions of power show a signal lack of vision. They don't 'lead' in any inspiring or creative sense of the word. In *The Paradox of Success*, John R O'Neil highlights this failure:

"…many leaders gradually close themselves off from new possibilities, rejecting experiences they come to consider inappropriate or activities that don't mesh with their self-image. This constriction of the possible could be the single largest obstacle in the way of renewal."

The "constriction of the possible" is a telling phrase to describe what many people think about those who hold sway over us. There is a general tendency to be reactive rather than proactive, to come up with short-term measures rather than long-term solutions, to respond to crises rather than take visionary action to prevent them.

"If we want to get out of the mess that we're in, then we must realise that our old solutions to problems, our old worn ideas of how things ought to work, are not going to get us there."

Marilyn Ferguson

In a society where, as we have seen, more decision-making power than ever before is in the hands of ordinary individuals, the traditional notion of leadership – dominance and control – is no longer desirable or acceptable.

"A leader has more external power – more ability to manipulate and control – than others.….That concept of leadership is not what individuals who are growing in authentic power gravitate toward or desire."

Gary Zukav

As more individuals grow in 'authentic power', an entirely different kind of leader is called for and coaching such new leaders is a rapidly growing area of the profession.

Personal responsibility?

"If more people knew what they felt about life and society, governments would have no choice but to respond."

Charles Handy

The problem is that many people don't know what they feel about "life and society". The all-pervading influences of business, politics and the media leave 'ordinary' individuals feeling powerless and confused. The

vast resources of the Internet are a mixed blessing. We have at our fingertips a huge mass of knowledge, more than our minds could ever compre-
hend, so we begin to believe that the answers are all there somewhere and
we can find them if we want to. But the deep, important questions
remain unanswered.

There is a large group of the population, including most of our leaders, who believe that life is predictable and controllable, linear and continuous where one thing leads to another in a reasonably straight line. Yet
all the time, life is proving us wrong, so we have the paradox of many people who are ready to take up their 'authentic power' but who are unsure
of the best way to use it.

We are told by Socrates that the unexamined life is not worth living
but as Antony de Mello notes:

> "Most people don't live aware lives. They live mechanical lives,
> mechanical thoughts – generally somebody else's – mechanical emo-
> tions, mechanical actions, mechanical reactions."

When those who are prepared to do so take time out to become more
'aware', they are often struck by feelings of frustration. They know things
could be better, not just for themselves but for their community, their
society and their larger world. But they don't know where to begin. The
temptation is for them to throw their hands up in despair and do nothing so it is not surprising that one of the major roles of the life coach is
to assist those who are willing to examine their lives and to start shaking
off their 'mechanical' chains.

The heart of the matter

Greater personal and individual choice
MINUS
Traditional framework and constraints
EQUALS
A need for new and different decision-making support.

When there is a lack of firm structure, there is more freedom but there is
also more personal responsibility. The onus has moved from the tribe to

the individual. To the question "Why do we need life coaches now when we haven't before?" the answer is to be found in the new choices we have to make now which we didn't before. Such choices are those that would previously not have been ours to make without the constraining influence of family, church and employer. Now that we can and should make them for ourselves, a different type of support structure is needed – the framework of a regular, focused, uniquely personal 'change facilitation service' or, in other words, a coach.

"The journey to tomorrow will be an off-road experience."

THREE

The skills of the coach

The heart of coaching consists of a series of conversations. As we have seen, these take place in an atmosphere of mutual trust and openness. The coach's role in these exchanges is to discover for herself and her client a whole body of information not previously accessible. This forms the raw material that the client uses to decide what he wants to create and what actions he wants to take. The information is elicited by the coach using a range of skills, of which the most vital are described below.

1. Listening

> "Real help, professionally or personally, consists of listening to people, of paying respectful attention to people so that they can access their own ideas first."
>
> Nancy Kline

The keystone of coaching is deep and attentive listening. This is not a passive skill. The client needs to be heard and to be heard completely. It is the coach's job to hear it all, to relate to it and to identify with it. The coach will be listening for a whole host of different elements – values, strengths, emotions, needs, blocks, fears, drives, assumptions. Above all, the coach will be listening for the truths that the client is not yet aware of himself. And she will be listening as much for what's missing as for what's said. For many clients, being listened to in this way is a rare and valuable experience.

The coach also has to be clear and firm about what will not be listened to so that the client gets full value from the coaching session. Only a short time is allowed for 'whinging' and for the convoluted relating of interactions of the "Then she said…and I said…and, would you believe it..." kind. As my first coach told me, "Keep your stories for your friends." Listening only to what is important in a coaching relationship sometimes means the coach has to interrupt and it is important that the client knows that this may happen and understands why.

The coach will be listening for certain give-away phrases like:

"I can't..."
"I know I should..."
"He ought to..."
"It's not fair..."
"No, I'm fine, really."
"But what will people think?"
"I'd love to, but...."
"I've got to be realistic." (For some reason, this always means pessimistic, not optimistic.)

Listening, of course, takes place in silence but may include prompts like "Tell me more about that", "What else do you think about this?" or a reflecting back for confirmation – "It sounds as if..."

A good coach listens with humility, being aware of her own reactions to what is being said and how these might cloud the issue, and knows when to move from listening to questioning and clarifying.

> "No-one has listened to me so patiently before... coaching gives me time and space to reflect and recharge my batteries."
>
> Helen, primary school teacher and coaching client

Listening is the best tool the coach has for assessing what her clients need from her as a coach and how far they are along the road of personal development.

"To 'listen' another's soul into a condition of disclosure and discovery may be almost the greatest service that any human being ever performs for another."

Douglas Steele, *A Random Harvest*

2. Questioning

If, as coaches believe, the client knows what's best for himself, then much of the coach's role will be to ask questions. This may sound easy but the skill of the coach lies in knowing what questions to ask, when to ask them and what to do with the answers. Sometimes an entire coaching session may take the form of questioning by the coach and answers from the client. The more powerful the questions, the deeper and more effective the coaching.

Strong questioning, followed by as long a period of silence as is needed, is the one thing most clients get nowhere else in their lives. People are used to hearing polite, non-committal queries and to giving shallow, acceptable answers. In a session with a coach, expect to be asked questions which stop you in your tracks and for which you have no ready reply.

Examples:

- "What are you putting up with?"
- "What are you most grateful for at this moment?"
- "What risks are you currently taking?"
- "How much of what you do really stretches you?"
- "How much money are you saving now?"
- "What do you see as the main block to your promotion?"
- "How can you use me as your coach to your best advantage?"
- "What does success mean to you?"
- "What do you really want?"
- "What's the most important thing in your life at the moment?"
- "What's the truth about this situation?"
- "What would you have to do to make this happen?"
- "What have you learned from this experience?"
- "So where do we go from here?"

"The brain that contains the problem also contains the solution –
often the best one."

Nancy Kline

Being constantly questioned about the things that really matter gets
under the client's skin until he begins to question himself in the same way
and looks for answers in the same place – inside himself.

3. Acknowledging

This is more objective than praise or compliments. It is quite simply the
coach putting into words something that she has noticed. This helps to
make the client more aware of what he has achieved and checks that he is
also appreciating his own progress. It is not flattery or patronising. It is
always unconditionally constructive, offering a combination of support
and approval.

When the coach notices growth, she will put it into words because
acknowledging it makes it more real for the client who may become aware
of it for the first time. Acknowledgement is not always easy for a client to
accept, particularly in the British cultural context of self-deprecation and
reserve. Learning to experience the power of simply being valued for what
you are is one of the many important by-products of having a coach.

Examples:

• "Congratulations, Kerry. You didn't give up – you just kept going."
• "I think you've made some huge changes over these last two months
  – how are you going to celebrate?"
• "You really had to work hard to get to this point in your career – it's
  paid off!"

Acknowledgement is crucial to the coaching relationship because it is
about who the client is, even when he doesn't recognise himself. It is also
a rare pleasure and so all the more valuable.

"Every day the world pulls us down, shakes us up, slices into us,
laughs at our attempts and belittles our triumphs. We legitimately
need to hear afresh every day a few things that are honestly good

about us. Most important of all, these good things will help us keep thinking for ourselves with courage and clarity."

Nancy Kline

4. Clarifying

Since life coaching is simply two people conversing, it can never be an exact science. From time to time, it becomes necessary for both coach and client to pause and ensure that both understand clearly what is being said. Even when the coach is speaking and articulating what she has heard the client say, it's not about the client being corrected or new words being put into his mouth. It's about both coach and client arriving together at precisely the same destination.

This helps to bring clarity and substance to what may seem to be an amorphous muddle. The coach articulates what she thought she heard and what she understood, 'saying it all and saying it straight'. When the client becomes clear about what he has conveyed to the coach, the way is open for new awareness and, in turn, for fresh possibilities and a shift in his belief about himself. All clarifying statements are likely to be short and crisp.

Examples:

- "So you've shifted from wanting to leave the company to wanting to stay in it but find a new role for yourself."
- "You seem to be telling me that your desire to travel is stronger than your desire to buy a home."
- "This is what I heard you say – you're proud of your children and you enjoy being a mother, but you don't feel valued because you haven't got a paid job."

Ensuring that the client is clear about what he is thinking and feeling is a crucial stage in the process of deciding what action to take next.

5. Focusing

One of the main tasks of the coach is to get the client to focus on what really needs attention. Many entrepreneurial clients have more ideas and projects than they can successfully develop. Some clients have a number of issues in their lives that they would like to be coached on. If the client tries to tackle too many things at once, the coaching becomes diffuse and little is achieved.

A good coach will encourage the client to focus on a maximum of three areas at a time and put everything else on hold. Even the three chosen may well be prioritised and taken one at a time. This enables coaching to take place in one designated area and for the client to see clearly what changes need to be made. Having a major impact on a single area can yield a multiplicity of results – the 80/20 rule. If the client has numerous problem areas and focus is put on the most troublesome 20%, the other 80% often disappear as a result.

Examples:

- "I know you've got lots of good ideas for your new business but let's explore which one will be the most marketable."
- "Which do you want to deal with first – your concerns about your son or your problem at work?"
- "Which three sources of income do you think will give you the most profit?"
- "You seem to have a lot of goals you want to achieve. Let's make a list of them now and then you can decide which one you want to go for first."

Sometimes the reason why clients come for coaching is that they feel overwhelmed by 'problems'. The coach understands that a 'quick fix' in one area can boost confidence both in the coaching process and in the client's own ability to sort things out.

6. Providing vocabulary

"They feel the unhappiness of their isolation and the emptiness of their 'togetherness'; they feel their impotence, the meaninglessness of their lives. Many feel all this very clearly and consciously: others feel it less clearly, but are fully aware of it when someone else puts it into words."

Erich Fromm

No one can clearly explain themselves if they don't have the appropriate words. A major responsibility of the coach is "to provide a new language that allows the client to make new observations." The coach's key tool is language. A professional coach is trained to be especially sensitive to the use of language, both in listening to it and in the choosing of their own words. Language is what coach and client have in common but the coach needs to understand the client's point of view and why he sees the world as he does. The coach can then give him new language to allow him to talk about things differently and motivate the client to continue learning such language for himself.

Many people in thriving societies are now reaching the top level in Maslow's Hierarchy – that of self-actualisation – but without having the language to describe it or the skills to profit fully from it. The subtlety of vocabulary goes hand in hand with personal development. A good coach will help the client to draw distinctions between pairs of almost-but-not-quite synonyms.

Examples:

➤ **strength versus power:**
The difference between being strong in yourself, not needing to compete versus having power 'over' someone or the power to do something.

➤ **goals versus 'shoulds':**
What you really want and where you set the agenda versus doing what you think you should on someone else's agenda.

➤ **hearing versus listening:**
Hearing is taking in what's behind the words and what the feelings are versus simply taking in what's being said.

➤ **shift versus change:**
A shift is a fundamental reorientation of who you are, what you see or how you deal with life versus simply deciding to do things differently.

Language includes vocabulary, distinctions, figures of speech like metaphors and similes, combinations of words and probably words for all kinds of emotions, situations and processes which are new and alien to many clients. For these clients, learning a new language and finding words for things they never even knew existed is a major benefit of coaching. Both coach and client find that progress is made by leaps and bounds when they both have the language to describe what they're thinking and feeling.

7. Visioning

> "Beneath the fear of being punished for thinking for themselves, most people have ideas that matter, ideas that would make a difference if they could be developed fully."
>
> Nancy Kline

A vision is what gives an individual identity and purpose, but it cannot be manufactured. You can't 'get' or even 'create' a vision. It comes to you. You attract it when you're fully committed to growing to your fullest potential. Having said that, it's still a major part of the coach's job to enlarge beyond recognition the client's view of what is possible and what the client is capable of achieving. Your vision is always bigger than your current 'reality'. Once the client has seen what his vision is, a huge gap is revealed for the client to grow into. It gives direction and purpose.

> "Still, most people do have some kind of dream or a vision. But they don't take it seriously. So they resign themselves to humdrum, everyday lives."
>
> Marilyn Ferguson

Examples:

- "What would your ideal life look like?"
- "Is there an idea or project that has always attracted you?"
- "What were you passionate about when you were young?"
- "Where would you like to be living in two years' time?"
- "How do you want to be remembered?"
- "What do you see as possible for the world?"
- "What seems to you to be a wasted opportunity in the world as it is today?"

Articulating the possibility of a vision shifts the client's perception of himself as much bigger and more valuable than he had perceived. A coach cannot force the client to get a vision, but she can open the doors of possibility and talk about the reality of a vision without embarrassment or false reserve. For the client who already has a vision that he is whole-heartedly committed to, a strong and experienced coach is the best partner to have.

> "A life of never-ending learning and renewal is guided by a compelling vision of how your life should be, what you want to spend your time doing – what is worth doing."
>
> John R O'Neil

8. Strategising

A strategy, as used here, is simply a method of producing a desired outcome. It involves identifying and using all the resources at the client's disposal to get what he wants or needs. It's a Game Plan that is developed by the coach and client together.

Many clients will have goals which involve more than one or two straightforward action steps. The goal is what they want to accomplish; the strategy is a combination of many different tools to achieve the goal. The key ingredients of a strategy are:

- The desired outcome
- A list of the resources needed
- An action plan or timetable
- A budget

With the right combination of these elements, the coach helps the client to build a structure within which the goal can be more quickly and less stressfully achieved. The coach will not produce the strategy herself but will support the client in the creation of a checklist and in the development of his own strategy. The clearer the goal, the easier the creation of the strategy becomes.

Creating a strategy is not just a necessity for reaching a complex goal; it is also a template for the client to use in other areas when the coach may not be present.

Examples:

- "You say you want to be self-supporting during your college course. What would you need to do for that to be possible?"
- "Now you're clear that you want to work in marketing, let's work out what steps you can take to find that first job."
- "You've decided you want to make this career change. What resources do you need to make the transition as painless as possible?"

9. Requesting

The evidence for the success of coaching is the actions of the client. The coach will encourage this productivity by asking the client, at the end of each session, what he intends to do. So requesting is different in degree from questioning, and is a gentler, quieter type of challenging. Requests can more easily be refused without any damage to the coach/client relationship. The coach is liable to make requests of the client at frequent intervals during the coaching sessions. If these requests are accepted, they may turn into action points for 'homework'.

When the coach makes a request, the client may accept, refuse or amend the request – "Yes, I'll do that" or "No, I don't want to do that" or "I can't make twenty sales calls but I'll do ten" or even "I'll do twenty sales calls, not ten." The client may sometimes ask for time to consider the request and the coach will ensure that no request is ever turned into a demand. If a request is refused, there may be some discussion about the consequences of the refusal, but the decision about the course of action to be taken always stays with the client. The client will have been prepared in the initial coaching sessions to expect requests for action and for regular reports on the progress made.

Examples:

- "If you're not in a position realistically to complete the report this week, what will you do to progress it?"

- "My request is that you draw up a detailed balance sheet for your personal finances. Will you do that?"
- "I'd like you to make a list of ten people who could help you with this."
- "I'm asking you to take one whole day off work next week and do exactly what you want."
- "I'd like you to do a thirty minute session of cycling or swimming every day next week. Will you commit to that?"
- "If you don't want to confront your boss directly about this yet, what can you do to prepare the ground?"

Hearing a reasonable request from the coach, while also retaining the power to refuse, allows the client to make manageable, realistic steps and to gain new energy from seeing real progress made.

10. Advising

Advice, in coaching parlance, is not 'What I think you should do' but an opinion, a piece of information or an explanation, packaged and personalised to be of maximum use to the client receiving it.

It is not the coach's role to give the client instructions. On the other hand, the coach is, or should be, a resource for the client and a repository of a great deal of useful information. The coach will have her own areas of expertise and in many cases, they are the very reason why the client has chosen this particular coach. To withhold what the coach knows and can recommend would then be less than full value for the client.

But advice, in the coaching relationship, is never just an objective piece of wisdom. It is always something the coach will offer in a way that encourages the client to consider himself and his circumstances in relation to the advice offered.

On occasions, the coach may offer advice but will always check first if the client wishes to hear it. Sometimes the client will specifically ask for advice, in which case the coach may offer examples of her own experiences and share her point of view. This is done in the context of the coach and the client working together in partnership. The coach may direct the client towards sources of greater information and expertise than she is personally able to offer.

Examples:

- "When I was in a similar position, this is what I found helped...."
- "Let's explore the options together."
- "I'm not an expert on this. Do you know someone who is?"
- "I'm not an expert on this, but I know someone who is."
- "May I tell you what I know has worked for others in a similar position?"
- "I don't have any first-hand experience of this, but I can tell you about someone who does...."
- "I'll tell you what I know about this...."
- "This is how I advised another client and this is what happened."

The client gains as much as possible from the coaching relationship if the coach is ready to share her wisdom in an empowering way. This enables the client to tap into a new resource which, with a skilled coach, will be continually growing and deepening.

11. Providing new perspectives

> "...the way we see the world at a particular moment determines the actions we take."
>
> James Flaherty

What the coach does is to help the client see his world in new ways, in ways that expand his perception and his sense of what's possible. This skill is one which, more than any other, calls for metaphors and pictures. It's the skill that encourages the client to look out of his box and see the box for the limiting object it is. It's the skill that takes the client up in a balloon to view the whole big landscape of life and how he fits into it.

Until the client can see things in a new way he is unlikely to have many new ideas for making changes or for moving forward. Coaching provides the client with a place in which to examine his current position and to discover new and different possibilities. If the client sees the box he is sitting in as the only box on offer, he is not going to try to escape. Once a new perspective is offered – "You're sitting in a box. There are plenty more boxes out there to choose from, but you'll only be able to see them by moving out of yours" – the client is able to take action.

The coach may use various means to help the client view things differently. One of these is The Perspective Game (see *Co-Active Coaching* p.136) in which the coach asks the client to write down every possible way of looking at the current situation or every possible next step they can think of. Each of these possibilities can then be examined and considered before any further decisions are made. This allows for a great number of different options to be considered, some possibly appearing very far-fetched or even foolish to the client, but nevertheless important for inclusion. Offering new perspectives has nothing to do with accepting limitations and everything to do with expanding horizons and encouraging huge visions.

Examples:

- "Imagine you're in your manager's shoes. What do you think he'd like to see happen?"
- "So you think this move abroad will disrupt your children's education. But looking at it from their point of view, what will they gain?"
- "You believe you have to do what your friends want in order to be liked. Might they respect you more if you had your own plans?"
- "You think if you leave your job, you won't find another one. What if you have to take that risk before you find the ideal job for you?"
- "You could approach the interview not as if you are being judged but as your chance to find out if they're the kind of people you would choose to work with."

"I can now 'see' so much, as though I have a clear windscreen and because I can see through my window, my view is so much clearer. I always seemed to be putting on my windscreen wipers before, because it got dirty so quickly. It is as though I have a special screen that no longer mists up or gets dirty!"

Martin, Classic car restorer, and coaching client

The opportunity to change our view of the world, to replace permanently the lens through which we observe things is one of the most productive experiences that coaching can provide.

> "Seeing the world from more than one perspective shows us how others see us, opens new windows on the world, and gives us more freedom of choice."

John R O'Neil

12. Challenging

> "The purpose of challenging is not to cause pain, but to cause gain."

The client does not expect the coach to make his life easier. He employs a coach who expects more of him than he does of himself. One of the purposes of the coaching service is to challenge the client's view of life and his perspective on it. Usually the first challenge a coach issues to the client is to take himself and his life seriously.

GREAT EXPECTATIONS + COMPASSION = CHALLENGE

The actions taken as a result of being challenged are the evidence of progress, so no coaching session is likely to pass without a challenge, be it ever so small, being issued from coach to client. This is what sets the pace and pushes the client into setting larger and more meaningful goals. Most clients relish a challenge because they know it's the way to make faster progress. The mark of a skilled coach is to walk the tightrope between being too soft (under-challenging) and being confrontational and aggressive (over-challenging).

Sometimes the challenge comes in the form of a question, a statement or as a directive prod. The coach will expect the client to give due consideration to the challenge before deciding whether to accept, reject or amend it. If the leap between the client's current position and the goal suggested is too great, the client may decide to offer a reduced action which will still lead in the right direction. Very occasionally, a huge leap may be needed – 'You can't cross an abyss in two small jumps.'

"Whenever we reach out to new adventures, we learn valuable lessons."

Diane Dreher

Occasionally the coach will issue a challenge to the client to stop the coaching session and do something right then and there – "Ring that prospective new customer that you've been telling me about, ask for the business and call me straight back when you've done it."

Getting weekly reports from the client is sometimes a challenge – it forces the client to review and acknowledge his achievements and to analyse what he's learnt from his failures. Some coaches will even challenge their clients on the value that they're getting from the coaching experience. But the biggest challenge for most people is to 'be yourself', and to be it not just some of the time but all of the time.

Examples:

- "Why don't you leave work on time?"
- "So now you've become aware of this, what are you going to do about it?"
- "What's the one thing you're putting off doing?"
- "What you need to do now is….When will you start?"
- "Are you really committed to this course of action?"
- "I believe you're a person who doesn't allow himself to be treated in this way."
- "So the next step would be to tell your manager that you need more flexibility in your working pattern and to give him an outline of your proposals. When's the best time to do this?"

It is impossible, and undesirable, for a coach never to challenge her clients. A good coach is not willing to tolerate anything less than the client's best efforts, while still being supportive and empowering.

"We never know how high we are
Till we are asked to rise
And then if we are true to plan
Our statures touch the skies."

Emily Dickinson

FOUR

From the outside in

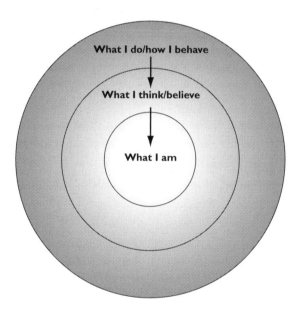

The majority of people initially come to coaching because they aren't sat-isfied with the peripherals of their lives – their jobs, their home, their rela-tionships with partner, family, colleagues or boss, their lack of time or money. Their discontent is focused on how they're experiencing the day-to-day externals of their life. When the coaching begins, however, they find that looking at such issues leads inevitably and inexorably into much deeper waters. Many are hoping that they will be told 'do this or that and everything will be fine'. It's true that the coach may well request some simple actions to be taken but there'll also be a lot of excavating into more profound matters – personal attitudes, needs and values – before any wide-reaching strategy is considered.

"We spend all our time and energy trying to change external circum-stances, trying to change our spouses, our bosses, our friends, our enemies, and everybody else. We don't have to change anything. Negative feelings are in you."

Anthony de Mello

Meaningful work

Many of us are resigned to the fact that finding and keeping a fulfilling job which pays a good salary is almost impossible and should not be expected. We hear a great deal about 'burn-out' – which at least implies some passion for the job, but just as many people suffer from what's been styled 'rust-out' – a gradual wearing away of our energy and creativity doing work which has little obvious value and without any recognition for our efforts. Although we don't expect a great deal from performing our work, we do expect more in the way of companionship. The break down of families and communities means that more of us are now seek-ing a sense of belonging in the workplace rather than where they live.

"We human beings…do not thrive without a sense of significance that we gain only by creating something we feel is of lasting value."

Sam Keen

If you're not happy with your current work situation, your coach will ask you what you really want. What do you want more of or less of? What do you enjoy about your present job and what do you dislike? What is your 'ideal job'? Is it to have a 'portfolio career' made up of different kinds of work? Full-time or part-time? Employed or self-employed? Examining the question of fulfilling work may not mean changing your job – it may mean changing your attitude or behaviour so that your current job becomes more satisfying.

"The real purpose of work is to give us an opportunity to practise being human – to discover everything we are and all that we can be, both as individuals and as members of a community."

Claude Whitmyer

Martin

Martin, a self-employed software designer, complained "I'm bored a lot of the time. I've tried to motivate myself but I can't seem to do it. I've chosen this work – so why am I not happy doing it?" With his coach he talked about finding out what he really wanted to do. She asked him powerful questions like "If you only had six months to live, what would you do?" and "If you didn't need to work for money, what work would you choose to do?" From thinking about the answers, Martin was able to formulate a much clearer idea of what kind of work really gave him a buzz. He was also asked to look in detail at all the jobs and clients he'd had in the past two years and to rate them on a scale from one to ten both for enjoyment and for the money he had earned from them. This exercise proved to be a real eye-opener for Martin who realised that a great deal of his work had just been routine and that many of his clients weren't paying him enough.

Martin and his coach together drew up a strategy for a more fulfilling worklife. This included increasing his fee rate by 50%, allowing Martin to eliminate those clients who offered only mundane work but to negotiate with others whose requirements he found more challenging. The rise in fees enabled him to work fewer hours and to spend the extra time on more creative and innovative projects of his own. He was able to break through the barrier of believing that he could never make enough money out of what he really enjoyed doing.

There is a perception that coaching in the workplace is chiefly for fast-track high-fliers, but it is actually a valuable tool for anyone who works for a living. Having a coach can be even more important for people in less senior positions because they may actually have the potential to be high-fliers without knowing it. Coaching can uncover a whole treasury of management and leadership material which would otherwise have gone undiscovered and unused.

> "A musician must make music, an artist must paint, a poet must write if he is to be ultimately at peace within himself. What a man can be, he must be. He must be true to his own nature."
>
> Abraham Maslow

Dealing with money and achieving financial independence

The whole subject of money is fraught with difficulties in our society. In many circumstances, it's not considered acceptable to talk about it, we don't learn much about it at school, we aren't taught how to budget or keep track of it. Money issues are numerous and widespread – deserving it, keeping it, investing it, attracting it, earning it, accepting it or being responsible about it. The one thing most people definitely know about money is that they never seem to have enough of it. A good coach will help to change a client's perspective to such an extent that he will never believe this to be true again.

Emma

Emma's whole life had been focused on reaching a goal – a well-paid job in marketing – and after couple of years, she found herself asking, "Is this it? Is this all there is to life?" When the opportunity arose to take voluntary redundancy, Emma was thrown into confusion. As she told her coach, "It's my chance to leave and do something completely different. But what if it doesn't work out?" What she really wanted to do was to be an interior designer but she had no training and no qualifications. The course she wanted to sign up for would take up most of her redundancy money and Emma was very risk-averse. "What if I'm no good at it? Or spend all that money and fail the exams?"

Because Emma's greatest fears were to do with money, her coach helped her to discover what her defining beliefs about money were. "That I'll never have enough of it. That there won't be enough to do the nice things in life, because only money buys happiness." Emma was challenged to produce the evidence for these beliefs but she was unable to do so. She discovered that she'd always had enough money to buy and do what she wanted, and paradoxically, she had been at her least happy when she had had plenty of money but no real contentment. With coaching, Emma was able to find new beliefs about money, based on her real life experience. What fitted was "I will always have enough money to meet my needs; my true talent can earn me money." With this new belief in mind, Emma started to work with her coach on devising a strategy for ensuring that she could take redundancy, sign up for the course and begin her career as a designer without any major financial concerns.

"Our most important financial asset is our own capacity to earn."

Stephen Covey

The one thing the coach knows for sure when a client claims he only wants coaching about his finances is – it's never just about money. As we have seen, coaching is focused on the 'Who' not the 'What', so your coach's first questions are likely to be about your attitude to money, not about your current financial position. A life coach is not (unless appropriately qualified) an expert on money. What your coach will do is encourage you to examine your relationship to money, decide what changes you want to make and how best to take action. She is likely to request that you find a good independent financial adviser and may be able to recommend one. Just as all the other coaching issues call for new awareness and learning, so does the subject of finance. You will be encouraged to take money matters seriously and to take your understanding of them to a new level.

 A story

The philosopher Diogenes was eating bread and lentils for supper. He was seen by the philosopher Aristippus, who lived comfortably by flattering the king. Aristippus said, "If you learnt to be subservient to the king, you would not have to live on lentils." Diogenes answered, "And if you learnt to live on lentils, you wouldn't have to grovel to the king.

Patrick

When he first came to coaching, Patrick, a self-employed computer consultant, was so stressed that he said he just felt like running away, though with a family to support he knew this wasn't a real possibility. He was in major financial trouble as an important client had gone bust, leaving a large invoice unpaid. On top of this, Patrick had allowed his accounts generally to get out of control and he now felt totally overwhelmed and unable to cope. "I don't actually know how I'm going to be able to afford your services," he admitted, "but I know I've got to get help from someone."

Through his coach's support and practical suggestions, Patrick was able to focus on one thing at a time – firstly getting his paperwork in order and then handing it over to an accountant. The next area to look at was the issue of bad debt and cash flow and getting low-cost interim finance through a contact recommended by his coach. They then worked out the best way to manage Patrick's relationships with the people to whom he owed money. Here he had a pleasant surprise. "I didn't realise how much goodwill they felt towards me," he reflected. "I just thought they'd be angry at having to wait for their money." It was a major learning point for Patrick that he needed to take a more active part in building strong links with his clients and that this would stand him in good stead in the future. Along with other improvements, like more delegation and better systems, Patrick was able to gain a great deal from his experience of being coached and he now makes it a habit to call on his coach whenever his business is going through a major transition.

A good life coach can help you to build your reserves of money and to adjust your spending and lifestyle to set you firmly on the road to financial independence.

A balanced life

> "Coaching can provide the accountability and support for those who want to pursue a simpler, slower, intentional lifestyle."
>
> Laura Whitworth et al

Getting a comfortable balance in their lives is often the first impulse for someone to come to coaching but even when other issues prevail, the question of living a balanced life is almost always somewhere in the background. Your coach may begin by asking you to consider how satisfied you are with the different areas of your life and how you feel about the balance between them. At the centre of everything will be your values – what is really important to you and what is non-negotiable.

The flower of life

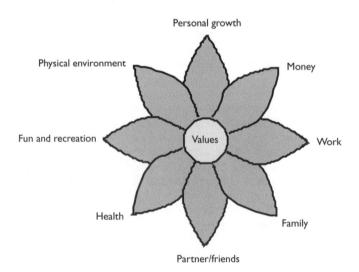

There are no hard and fast rules about balance. The important thing is to get it right for you, and it is not something that is settled once and for all. It's a process, not a destination. At different ages and stages of their lives, people need to vary the focus on the individual areas of their lives. Changes made in one area often have a beneficial effect on another. If you decide to concentrate on enhancing your physical environment, it is likely that your health will also improve.

Susie

When she decided to employ a coach, Susie's main area of concern was getting the balance right between the time she and her partner spent on refurbishing their old country property and the time they needed to spend together to nourish and deepen their relationship. "I thought it would all work out by itself but it's becoming so difficult. I'm not working at the moment so it's my job to do most of the DIY but when James comes home from his job, he's tired, criticises what I've done and we end up arguing."

Her coach advised Susie to see the house and her relationship as two different issues so that she could get a new perspective on both. Together they worked out a strategy for alternating her focus: one weekend to be for socialising and going out together, the next to work together on the house. James was somewhat sceptical about this plan and Susie had to control herself while she explained calmly that it was important to her to at least give it a try. After a few weeks, James admitted that it was good to have time together and to be doing the house as a joint project rather than feeling it was something Susie was doing just for herself. Susie realised she also benefited from giving herself permission to do no decorating at all on her weekends off. She reflected with surprise, "I'm getting on further with the house although I'm spending less time on it. And the arguments are definitely on the way out!"

Through coaching, you will be encouraged to explore and plan how to get the right lifestyle for you. This will probably include setting boundaries for yourself and others – going home from work on time, saying No to some demands, saying Yes to offers of help. An important area of balance for many people is to begin simplifying and de-cluttering their lives. There is also the importance of finding time for yourself. Your coach may ask you to complete a pie chart in which you estimate how much of your time is spent in different activities or in the different roles you play. You may also be asked to draw a pie chart that would represent your ideal work/life balance.

A story

The philosopher Socrates believed that a wise person would instinctively lead a frugal life. He himself would not even wear shoes; yet he often visited the market and would spend some time looking at all the goods for sale. When one of his friends asked why, Socrates said, "I love to go there and discover many things I am perfectly happy without."

"Why do we make such clear distinctions between work and play in our lives, often finding it difficult to bring the same quality of joy and attention to our work as we do to our leisure? And what do we miss out on by holding these attitudes?"

Rick Fields

Improving relationships and interpersonal skills

There's a paradox connected with the gaining and maintaining of healthy relationships – the less you need others, the more attractive you become to them. There is nothing more off-putting to many people than an aura of desperation about the person who longs for a long-term partner or who is searching for that one 'best friend'. One of the hardest truths for many coaching clients to learn is that 'selfishness' is the first priority for having good relationships in your life. Your coach will insist that you concentrate on taking care of yourself, feeding and exercising your body well, getting your own needs met and working towards achieving what you really want.

How can this focus on oneself possibly be a magnet for others? Because someone who values and cares for himself, to the extent that he is not 'needy' but can concentrate on the needs of others, is an unusual and attractive person. Because he has listened to and acted on his own needs and is fulfilling his own potential, he carries with him a joy and brightness that is infectious. Who would you rather spend your time with? Someone who is desperate for your attention, talks mainly about his woes and demands your sympathy? Or someone who is so at ease with himself that he has all the time in the world to listen to you and be with you, but who will not tolerate your self-sabotage and is very clear where his values and priorities lie? He is your friend or your partner because he chooses to be, not because he needs to be. With your coach's stringent questioning, you will probably discover very quickly if what you offer others is what you yourself would want to be offered.

> "Being able to manage emotions in someone else is the core of the art of handling relationships."
>
> Daniel Goleman

Lucia

In her forties, Lucia was still very much under the control of her elderly mother, who was increasingly becoming more demanding and less independent. In addition, her mother was always putting Lucia down and undermining her confidence. "She always notices things in the house that haven't been cleaned properly or she sees something I've bought and ticks me off for being extravagant. She's even starting to say hurtful things about my appearance. I'm beginning to dread her visits."

Coaching helped Lucia to see that she couldn't change her mother's behaviour but she could take responsibility for her own. She realised that she did not have to play the victim but could make changes in her relationship with her mother. Her coach challenged Lucia to stand up for herself and to improve her communication with her mother. Lucia practised role-playing the situation with her coach, finding the right words and tone of voice.

As a result, Lucia was able to explain to her mother that the criticisms were hurting her and, to protect herself, she would no longer listen to them. She stated quite calmly that she would simply walk away if her mother did not stop. When she had important things to do and her mother was making demands on her time for trivial matters, Lucia took control and stood her ground. She soon started to feel less oppressed and more in control of her emotions. In response, her mother became less needy and regained some of her independence.

To many people the idea of choosing the people in your life and forming your own community is a novel idea. We cannot choose the family we're born into and for some of us, the family we're given is not the one we'd select for ourselves. But our friends and the people we spend time with are resources which we have a great deal of control over. The American life coach Laura Berman Fortgang talks of 'three kinds of friends – those who sink you, those who float you and those who rocket you.' It is often time and money well spent to clarify with your coach how many friends you have in each of these three categories and what action you can take to decrease the first and increase the third. This doesn't mean that your coach will encourage you to ditch your oldest pals – rather she will help you to plan and take action on setting boundaries so that the people you spend most of your time with are those who inspire, motivate and delight you.

Tara

Living openly as a lesbian, Tara found that meeting and keeping friends who accepted her for herself was not easy. Many of her old acquaintances had distanced themselves from her. She came to coaching for the express reason to build up a community of supportive people around her. She explained to her coach that she had tried looking for friends in gay bars and clubs but had been disappointed. "The people in that sort of place only seem to want a sexual partner, not the sort of friendship I'm looking for." Her coach asked Tara, "Is your sexuality your most important value?" She realised that in the matter of friendship, it was not.

Tara was able to broaden her view of herself and to pinpoint exactly what she needed from the people she spent her leisure time with. After questioning from her coach, Tara was clear that she wanted friends who shared her interest in history, who enjoyed a serious discussion but who were also ready to have a 'fun time with a good giggle'. Her coach asked, "So where might you find such people?" With her coach's encouragement, Tara joined a club which organised talks and outings to historical houses, started an evening class to learn heraldry and signed up as a volunteer at the local museum. She began to meet exactly the sort of people she had been looking for and the kind of friendships she longed for began to develop.

"..when we are in this state of being where we are open to life and all its possibilities, willing to take the next step as it is presented to us, then we meet the most remarkable people who are important contributors to our life."

Joseph Jaworski

Dealing with failure and learning from experience

"Experience is not what happens to a man; it is what a man does with what happens to him."

Aldous Huxley

Laura Berman Fortgang cites failure as her main motivation for becoming a world-renowned coach. She is open about her original dream to succeed in the world of acting, in which she was reasonably successful. But when, by her late twenties, she had not achieved anything really outstanding, she became depressed and near to breakdown. From this depth of despair, she coached herself to look at things differently and to build herself a new life.

> "If you do not choose to create consciously, you will continue to create the same painful experiences that you have created previously. You will continue to do that until, in this lifetime or another, you understand the origin of the pain that you are experiencing. Then you will change. The change will be thorough, complete, and permanent."
>
> Gary Zukav

Angela

Angela is an intelligent, self-sufficient woman who prides herself on her ability to cope. As the mother of two small children, she became frightened and ashamed when her husband started to use violence against her while openly conducting an affair with another woman. She realised that divorce was the only answer, yet she also saw it as a humiliating public admission of failure. Her coach encouraged Angela to develop a positive vision of her future with the children rather than getting bogged down in her view that everything was collapsing. He also challenged her to 'have the best divorce ever' – a completely new perspective of events, which changed her perception from one of complete failure to one of a new, different relationship with her husband, both of them working together to get the best result for their children.

The coach will often give events which the client labels 'failures' a new slant, looking on them as experiments which had an unexpected outcome. Looking on failure simply as an opportunity for learning is still alien to our culture.

> "The advantages of stepping aside for a clear appraisal of progress seem obvious. Why is it so hard for many to do?…Too often our experiences of self-observations are harsh judgements when benign, forgiving eyes are appropriate."
>
> John R O'Neil

This 'clear appraisal of progress' is so much easier with a coach, when together you review what's happened and what you have learnt. Having a coach does not guarantee that you never fail, but it does ensure that, if failure occurs, you have constant, compassionate support and encouragement to learn as much as possible from the experience. Your coach will help you to investigate exactly why you failed and help you to take action – to 'rescue' the failure or to learn from it and do things differently in future. If you learn your lesson well, and keep your coach, you need never go through that particular failure again.

Joanna

Joanna had applied for a promotion within the organisation she had worked for happily for several years. It was a couple of levels above her current position but a job which she knew she could do well. At her interview, she was told that unfortunately, although she had plenty of experience, she didn't have the necessary qualifications. She felt angry and humiliated, particularly since no appointment was made and the vacancy was partly filled by Joanna herself taking on extra work. She turned to a life coach for help in making the decision to leave. "I feel there's no other choice – the senior managers only see me as a supervisor. I'm sure my boss thinks the same as they do. I'll have to start again somewhere else."

Through the coaching sessions, Joanna started to see that what she thought of as a major setback could be viewed as a challenge to prove herself. Together they worked out a plan to ensure that Joanna was offered the job. The tactics included getting her boss on her side, telling him what she thought she could bring to the job and asking him to act as her mentor. He helped her to rewrite her CV to bring it more into line with the job specification and to highlight the positive aspects of Joanna's experience within the company. Joanna's final challenge was to persuade the senior managers to reconsider their decision. Knowing they were unable to fill the position from outside, they agreed to a second interview. After role playing the interview with her coach, Joanna was able to persuade them that she was perfectly capable of doing the job and, if offered it, was prepared to undertake training to gain the qualifications she lacked. The managers were so impressed by her enthusiasm and perseverance that they offered her the job on the spot.

 *A story*

I was a revolutionary when I was young and all my prayer to God was 'Lord, give me the energy to change the world.' As I approached middle age and realised half my life was gone without my changing a single soul, I changed my prayer to, 'Lord, give me the grace to change all those who come in contact with me. Just my family and friends, and I shall be satisfied.' Now that I am an old man and my days are numbered, my one prayer is, 'Lord, give me the grace to change myself.' If I had prayed for this right from the start I should not have wasted my life.

"The defining characteristic of being human is recidivism – we backslide, that's our nature. We train, investigate, and we fall back a bit. This is not a sin, this is how we are, and gradually, through trial and discovery, we may find ways of being that are more satisfactory."

Steven D. Goodman

FIVE

From the inside out

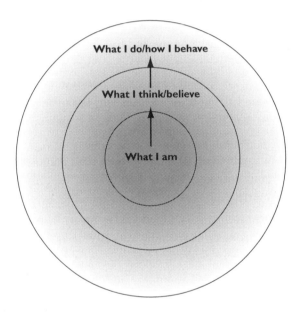

There are no 'standard' examples of what people gain through coaching. Every one is individual and unique, but there are broad brushstrokes to be painted of areas in which many people have found life coaching of lasting and unexpected value. The chief benefit of having a coach is that you begin to lead an 'examined' life. You will discover very quickly that the transformation of your life is likely to be unstoppable. With your coach, you may decide to work on specific issues at first, and this may build later into a complete life plan.

Self-awareness

> "A nice definition of an awakened person is a person who no longer marches to the drums of society, a person who dances to the tune of the music that springs up from within."

Anthony de Mello

Becoming more self-aware isn't a process that demands any special qualities or intelligence. For many clients it is not an easy or comfortable process. Even the apparently simple step of deciding to employ a coach raises issues which you may never have considered before. It upsets things, it puts extra pressure on us when we find out things we'd rather not know. It takes courage to accept the truths about yourself that you may have been suppressing. What is even riskier is to question your deepest beliefs and assumptions and to be open to 'thinking the unthinkable'. Nobody wants to discover that the foundations on which they've based their life so far are shifting sands.

So if it's so difficult, why bother? Why is it so important to become more aware of your real self? Firstly, because it's the only way in which you can fundamentally take control of your own life, even though at first it seems as if you're losing your life as you've know it. Secondly, because only by really knowing yourself can you live your life as you're truly meant to. You become an awakened person. You will find yourself getting more in touch with your own feelings. This has been the subject of much derision in many, mainly masculine, areas of society. One reason for this is that the most prevalent emotions in our society are pain and fear. Why should we want to become more sensitised to these? Another reason is that we are not taught the language of emotions and the fine distinctions between them. Most of us have more words to describe the colours of paint when we consider home-decorating than labels for the whole range of emotions from love to hate and from joy to sorrow. While developing your sensitivity to your emotions, you will also be extending your vocabulary with which to describe them.

> "…we must look at the lens through which we see the world, as well as at the world we see,….the lens itself shapes how we interpret the world."

Stephen Covey

Sue

Sue, a very able solicitor in her late 20s, was fuming at her treatment at work. "I do a huge amount of work in record time but I don't get any praise or even acknowledgement for this." She complained that it had been the same in her previous job and she wasn't prepared to put up with it again. This fact alerted Sue's coach to the possibility that there may be something about the way Sue behaved or reacted at work that exacerbated the situation. Through coaching, Sue began to realise that she had a real need to be cared for and to be recognised, yet she was working in a very male-oriented environment where showing concern and giving praise were not considered important. Her colleagues thought it obvious that she was doing her job well and didn't feel the need to say so. Gaining this insight made a difference. Once Sue understood what her needs were, and that she was unlikely to get them met at work, she stopped ranting about the unfairness of it all. She found appreciation elsewhere, through her friends and family.

Sue was also largely unaware of how she came across to others. She had a way of correcting people that was somewhat abrupt and stern, as if she were undeniably right and the other person hopelessly wrong. Through role-playing, her coach was able to hold up a mirror to herself so that she saw herself more clearly. Sue was a quick learner. By softening her communication style, she found she was treated more graciously in return. This produced a real shift in Sue's perception of herself and she was able to apply her self-knowledge in many other areas of her life.

No human being can function without feelings. It's vital to acknowledge the importance of our emotions – something which many of us have been taught to be wary about and not to allow into decision-making equations.

Terry

Now in his early forties, Terry had worked for a large advertising agency for sixteen years. Most of his colleagues were considerably younger than he was and he was beginning to feel that his face didn't fit any more. "A new manager has just been appointed," Terry told his coach, "and he told me that if I didn't improve my performance, my job would be on the line." He was worried that if redundancies were necessary, he'd be the first to go and at his age, finding another position in this business would be almost impossible.

Through his coach's questioning and clarification, Terry discovered he was a perfectionist; he needed to double-check everything and wasn't as flexible as his manager required. He also foresaw problems before the others and reported these to his manager. Terry began to see how his manager perceived him – as negative and a bit of a wet blanket. His coach challenged Terry to say something positive to the others in his team about himself and his job every day for a week. In the following week, he was to go to his manager at least twice with solutions rather than problems. As a further means of creating a more favourable impression, Terry was able to have a chat with his manager, asking how he was getting on in his new job and if there was anything Terry could help him with. A better relationship grew up between them and Terry found ways in which his attention to detail could be used to the team's advantage.

The process of becoming self-aware is only the beginning. Through the sessions with your coach, you will learn more about yourself but only through new actions and behaviour, by putting yourself into unfamiliar situations and giving yourself new experiences, will you also get a new perception of your role in the world.

However, the whole process is fraught with danger because it inevitably wakes up within us all the impulses which oppose such an awakening. Enter the gremlins!

Recognising and defeating 'gremlins'

"What you are aware of you are in control of; what you are not aware of is in control of you. You are always a slave to what you're not aware of."

Anthony de Mello

Many of us are not aware of how powerful are the forces which hold us back, even once we have taken a conscious decision to make changes and move forward. These forces most often appear as quiet but insistent voices in our head. These inner voices have been caught, pinned down and dissected brilliantly by Richard Carson in *Taming Your Gremlin*.

"Your gremlin is the narrator in your head…He is with you when you wake up in the morning and when you go to sleep at night…He wants you to accept his interpretations as reality, and his goal from moment-to-moment, day-to-day is to squash the real, vibrant you within."

The picture of some of the most difficult barriers that people need to overcome as nasty little creatures in control of your mind is a godsend when talking about the things that hold us back. And – here's the bad news – as soon as you become more aware, you rouse "…that inner voice that abhors change and demands the status quo."

So what exactly are gremlins and why do they have such power? They are the hardcore of all the up-bringing, conditioning, brain-washing and 'education' you have experienced since you were born. They are an amalgam of all the 'shoulds' and 'shouldn'ts', 'musts' and 'mustn'ts' and 'ought tos' you have heard since childhood.

Think about how you were brought up – where was the emphasis? Was it: 'Have a go. Try it and see. Don't worry about failing. It doesn't matter what other people think. You're special. You can do anything you want.' Or was it: 'Be careful. Don't hurt yourself. Don't show off. Wait till your father gets home. You'll never make anything of yourself. Think what the neighbours would say. Just do what you're told.' Probably somewhere between the two extremes. But somehow the negative seems to have a more powerful and lasting effect. The gremlins are born, nurtured and thrive, because what we crave for is love. For most of us, the outward sign of love is its pale and second-rate cousin – approval. Thus we are conditioned to become addicted to approval.

> "Now this is exactly what your society did to you when you were born. You were not allowed to enjoy the solid, nutritious food of life – namely, work, play, fun, laughter, the company of people, the pleasures of the senses and the mind. You were given a taste for the drug called approval, appreciation, attention."
>
> Anthony de Mello

So when you talk about 'I' and 'What I feel' and 'What I think', there is probably not a great deal of 'I' involved, but plenty of parents, teachers, relations, friends, and assorted figures of authority. The gremlins represent other people's agendas. There may be nothing wrong with some of what the gremlins say – a certain amount of it may be good sense and reflect your own values. But until you hear the gremlins speak, and recognise them for what they are, you will never know which ones to listen to and which to ignore.

Clare

Clare, aged 23, was good at her job and had previously enjoyed her work as a personal assistant, but found her new boss hard to cope with. He was easily angered and seemed to have very little understanding of, or interest in, other people's feelings. "He communicates mainly by emails," Clare complained, "and when he does talk to me directly, he's rude and abrupt." After discussing it with her coach, Clare began to realise that she was allowing herself to be treated in this way because all her 'gremlin' messages were telling her she had to be pleasant, she should respect her boss, she ought to put up with it. "I feel it's my fault – he puts me in the wrong all the time."

Through coaching, Clare decided that being senior did not give anyone permission to behave badly towards her. She was able to start setting some limits around how she allowed herself to be treated and, role-playing with her coach, she practised saying to her boss, calmly but firmly, things like "When you speak to me like that, I feel put down and humiliated. Can we discuss how to communicate better? I would like you to talk to me more considerately."

Clare found it really hard to say these things face to face with her boss – her gremlins were fighting it all the way! But once she had plucked up the courage to do so, she was surprised at the results she got. Her boss was not a completely changed character but he did become a great deal more respectful in his dealings with her and, Clare noticed, with other people as well. She was later asked to carry out a project into in-house communication styles which not only boosted her confidence further but also gave her a whole new range of skills.

When you change your behaviour, you may cause others to change. If you change one thing in your life, other things change automatically.

> "Modern man is ready to take great risks when he tries to achieve the aims which are supposed to be 'his', but he is deeply afraid of taking the risk and responsibility of giving himself his own aims."
>
> Erich Fromm

Listening to gremlins is like painting inside the lines of a child's colouring book. All that this reveals is whether you can successfully stay within the lines that someone else has drawn. Rejecting them and listening to yourself means you create your own paintings from scratch – it's much more exciting and will reveal far more of your true self.

> "The purpose of authority in our lives is to outgrow it."
>
> Nancy Anderson

Jack

Jack, an independent financial adviser, came to coaching stressed and tense, but when asked why, replied, "Just the usual niggles." The niggles were indeed minor – matters at work that were getting on his nerves, some irritating things his wife did – but they still caused Jack to feel wound up. This was made worse by Jack's opinion that he was 'overreacting' and 'shouldn't' feel as he did. Jack was also bothered by the fact that he loved to play golf but felt he 'shouldn't' do it at the weekend because it took him away from his family. He couldn't play during the week because he 'should' be working. His coach helped him to become aware of these messages.

They didn't spend much time examining why Jack felt as he did – the origin of the 'gremlins' was much less important than dealing with them. Through coaching, Jack was able to accept that it was irrelevant whether he 'should' or 'shouldn't' feel as he did. They were his feelings and he began to own them. When he accepted who he was and what he wanted, he became kinder to himself and opened up more to his wife. He was surprised to discover that she was perfectly happy for him to play golf at the weekend. Jack then realised that he did not need to obey the gremlin voices. Rather he could decide which ones he agreed with and ignore those he didn't.

"One of the primary functions of the coach is to help the client improve the internal dialogue he carries around with him and that influences how he learns and performs when the coach isn't around."

Timothy Gallwey

Working with a coach can be revelatory – you begin to recognise and name your particular gremlins. You give yourself space and time in which to listen critically to their voices and to decide for yourself which ones are worth keeping and which you have outgrown. More importantly, your coach acts as a reliable partner in the fight to defeat the gremlins that are holding you back. The ultimate aim is that your 'internal dialogue' be supportive at all times.

Restoring integrity and honouring values

Once you have begun to realise how much of what you believe, think and do has very little connection with your own self, the question of integrity is raised. Integrity here means what is right or healthy for you, not what is right or wrong in an abstract moral sense. You may be out of integrity if you're working at the wrong job or socialising with the wrong people.

'Wrong' here doesn't mean there's anything intrinsically wrong with the job or the people, just that they're not right for you. It means telling the truth and living exactly 'who you are'. The state of being in integrity means taking complete responsibility for all you do or choose not to do and is ultimately the only sure way to consistent feelings of peace and well-being.

Donald

In the past three years, Donald had changed companies twice. Now in his third job, he was feeling his old dissatisfaction at work. His coach discovered that Donald's feelings of frustration had been similar in all his jobs. Her first request of him was that he undertake an exercise which would help him to discover his core values; the things that he considered to be most important in life.

When Donald identified his top five values, he found they included creativity, independence and adventure. He was shaken to realise that, while he was doing his job, his values were hardly involved at all. It gave him a new perspective on his difficulties at work and allowed him to consider a complete change of career.

As we have seen, we are not encouraged to be truthful or to show our real selves in public. We put on a 'persona' that is more acceptable if we want to gain approval. We become what Daniel Goleman calls 'social chameleons' who:

> "...don't mind in the least saying one thing and doing another, if that will win them social approval. They simply live with the discrepancy between their public face and their private reality."

Coaching helps you to identify and live by your values. Your coach will work with you to discover what your personal values really are so that you are able to act, to quote Goleman again, "in accordance with your deepest feelings and values no matter what the social consequences."

Julian

Julian was the managing director of a company that formed part of a group in the financial services industry. There had been a change in the leadership of the group and the new leader was very different in approach and motivation. Julian's coach helped him to see that he had the choice of carrying on as before, with the likelihood of conflict, or changing his style to match the new leader. Together they worked on a variety of techniques to give Julian the confidence and style of behaviour he needed. However, eventually his coach sensed that Julian had reached the point where, if he carried on adapting, he would be betraying his integrity. "We need to look at your life in general and clarify what you value, and then compare it with what your company values. Then we can ask how far you are prepared to bend."

One of Julian's core values was a measured, analytical approach to decision-making, but the company ethos now valued rapid, intuitive decision-taking. Julian came to realise there was too big a mismatch. He asked the coach "What should I do?" but the reply was firm: "Coaching is about guiding people to their own solutions. I've helped you explore the options, but you have to make the decision."

"Self-esteem is built by expressing our potential, by 'knowing who we are', by being authentic with ourselves and one another; no longer by trying to prove anything to others but be being true to one's own best standards."

Richard Bolles

Making better decisions and changes

People often begin the coaching process with the idea that certain things cannot be changed. When asked "Can you imagine your ideal life?" the response is often "Oh, yes, but of course it's not realistic to expect that." It's as though we are trained not to expect too much – that way we won't be disappointed.

"..no matter how much of our life we perceive to be unchangeable, because it is always in the control of someone or something else, there is always that part that is under our control, and that we can work on to change. Be it 2%, 5%, 30% or whatever, it is almost always more than we think."

Richard Bolles

Maureen

Maureen had approached her new job with enthusiasm but six months later, she complained to her coach that everything was moving too slowly. Disillusioned by the difficulties of trying to operate in a much more laid-back culture, she was already thinking of leaving. "I've got to get out of this place. I feel like an isolated pool of energy, drying up. It's just so frustrating."

Her coach helped her to recognise a different perspective. "This is a challenge for you. The source of your frustration at work is also potentially the source of your satisfaction." Maureen realised that if she couldn't single-handedly change the culture, she could instead change the way she reacted to it. She understood that she could decide to stay and take on the challenge of becoming a catalyst – a leader instead of a leaver. She used her coaching sessions to work out a strategy for achieving this.

"A great number of our decisions are not really our own but are suggested to us from the outside; we have succeeded in persuading ourselves that it is we who have made the decision, whereas we have actually conformed with expectations of others, driven by the fear of isolation and by more direct threats to our life, freedom and comfort."

Erich Fromm

The gremlins are at work again! The role of the gremlin in decision-making is powerful if not recognised and checked because the gremlin imposes its own set of rules. The gremlin either wants the status quo – "Change is the Gremlin's enemy" – or as little boat-rocking as possible. Decisions are made which cause the least upheaval to others or the least discomfort for the decision-maker. The most important life decisions need values not gremlins at their heart, whatever the consequences, because in the long term, only honouring values will bring true fulfilment. You and your coach together will check the authenticity of your choices – are they consistent with your stated values and your integrity?

"Being trusted with making choices and being encouraged to use our own skills are crucial to building that vital quality, self-esteem, which leads to confidence, self-reliance and self-motivation."

John Whitmore

Nikki

Nikki was reeling from the experience of having just been made redundant. The firm she was working for had been taken over and during the restructuring her post had been amongst the casualties. Nikki hired a coach who suggested that she resist the temptation to rush and find another job, at any cost. Nikki identified with this feeling strongly. She agreed to use this period productively and began to list the benefits of having some extra time. With this overview in place she was able to take stock of her long-term situation.

With her coach, Nikki had been working on her assertiveness skills and self esteem. The crunch came when Nikki's former employer contacted her to see if she would be prepared to return to work on a contract basis. The conditions were not favourable, so Nikki found herself negotiating. Finally her fees were raised to within the parameters she had set and the commission basis was changed in her favour. "Coaching has been an enormous help," observed Nikki, "Without it, I know I'd have panicked, rushed into finding any job – probably the wrong one. Knowing I didn't have to accept the conditions gave me a lot more confidence to negotiate my own terms."

It is important to work out a strategy with your coach and take small, measurable risks so that you move out of your comfort zone slowly. If your commitment wavers, "the coach will stand fast rather than participate in the retreat."

> "Do you have the patience to wait
> till your mud settles and the water is clear?
> Can you remain unmoving
> till the right action arises by itself?"

From the Tao Te Ching

Seeing the present as 'perfect'

> "An Italian poet said, 'We live in a flash of light; evening comes and it is night forever.' It's only a flash and we waste it. We waste it with our anxiety, our worries, our concerns, our burdens."

Anthony de Mello

Talking about death is something we are encouraged to fear and avoid. But without a deep realisation of how transient our life is, we cannot hope to make the most of the life we have been given. You would probably resist vigorously if you were asked to accept the idea that your present life is perfect. But if the only alternative were death, you'd be likely to agree that life was, after all, very precious exactly as it is. Even more than money, death is a taboo subject in our society. But if you have a life coach, the subject may well have to be broached. Not because we coaches are a morbid lot, but simply because our business is that most vital of things – life. You simply cannot talk profoundly about life without acknowledging, however briefly, that it is finite and that death is real.

"It's only in looking at our lives from the end that we can begin to determine what's really important for us and what is only distraction and waste. The sooner we begin to see life in this light, the better, because at the end of your life it will be too late."

James Flaherty

Some clients come to coaching because they've had life-changing experiences or traumas that brought them up short and caused them to re-evaluate how they were living their lives. Why wait for an experience like this to make changes? How would you like your obituary to read? What would you want engraved on your tombstone?

"So imagine you're lying flat and you're dead. Now look at your problems from that viewpoint. Changes everything, doesn't it?"

Anthony de Mello

Pippa

"I've always wanted to be a writer. I used to scribble stories while I was at school and actually came second in a competition with one of them. My parents insisted that I go to college and get some qualifications – secretarial, of course! They couldn't believe I would be able to support myself financially by my writing and to be fair, the skills I learnt have been very useful. Now I'm in my early 30s, I'm married with two small children and I'm beginning to feel really frustrated. I work part-time in a local hotel – the work is pretty mundane but at least I get out of the house and meet people. I'm always writing stories in my head about the guests at the hotel! I'm lucky that my mother lives nearby and looks after the children, but this isn't what I planned to do with my life. I'm longing to write a proper novel, a best seller – I know I could do it, but how on earth do I fit that in with my family responsibilities? My children and husband have to come first. I just get so depressed sometimes thinking about my boring life."

When Pippa got herself a coach, she had expected to be motivated and helped in reorganising her life to find a better job and more childcare. But in the early sessions with her coach, she was surprised to find herself thinking deeply and questioning her discontent. She recalled how precious her own childhood had been and how much she had loved the time she spent with her mother. She began to see how she could change her attitude more easily than she could change her life. She started to look on her job as 'raw material' for her writing and made sure she wrote down everything she wanted to remember. Her coach encouraged her to draw up a plan for the completion of her first novel in two years' time. She and her husband worked out a strategy which allowed Pippa a regular chunk of time every weekend when she would be completely free to write. On reflection Pippa understood how her coach had challenged her to transform her view of herself from a bored and frustrated housewife into a novelist with an important project and a deadline.

"Mindfulness is attunement to today's demands to avoid tomorrow's difficulties."

Ellen Langer

In much self-development material, there is a great deal of emphasis on setting and achieving goals. This is often the initial spur to take action and is necessary to feel we're making progress, but goals are only the beginning. Laura Berman Fortgang's vivid picture for this is that goals are like stabilisers on a child's bicycle. When you're a beginner, you need them to learn how to ride, but eventually, when you are experienced in living your life as it's meant to be, you take them off and don't even notice they're gone.

"The achievement of goals is important. But the real juice of life, whether it be sweet or bitter, is found much less in the product of our efforts than in the process of living itself, in how it feels to be alive."

George Leonard

Jeremy

Jeremy was discontented with his work but couldn't decide what he needed to do to improve it. He told his coach, "It's my boss – he's a control freak. He watches over me constantly. He always wants to know what I'm doing. I'm really good at my job but he never gives me any praise. I feel angry and demoralised." Jeremy's coach asked him to think of something he admired about his boss. Jeremy was taken aback – "The man's an idiot – what else can I say?" But after further pressure from his coach, Jeremy grudgingly admitted, "He's very logical and good on detail. He's also articulate."

Through coaching, Jeremy began to appreciate that he needed to see how he could improve things as they were at present, not just get stuck in complaining mode. His coach told Jeremy, "You can begin to change the negative dynamic by being the first to start the process. Tell your boss what you admire about him." Jeremy rose to the challenge and was able to report, "I really felt something shift when I told him how good he is at logical, detailed work. He was obviously pleased and things have felt a lot easier since then. He's certainly not on my back in the way he used to be."

Of course you can improve things for yourself without investing in a coach. But it will be a long hard slog and you'll often be tempted to give up. If you travel the journey with a coach as your companion, it isn't necessarily less difficult, but you get longer-lasting results much more quickly. Joan Borysenko describes this sense of the present being perfect as:

> "A feeling of connectedness. For me, that experience always brings forth a tremendous sense of gratitude. The recognition that life is a tremendous mystery and a tremendous gift and that we are most fortunate to be living it."

SIX

Coaching in the workplace

It's important to distinguish clearly between life coaching as described so far, and coaching at work, which has many similar characteristics but a more narrowly focused outcome. The usual purpose of coaching in the workplace is to enhance the performance of the employee. Of course, this may include encouraging the employee to fulfil his potential and to build self-awareness but the most common reason for offering coaching to people at work is to ensure that the organisation concerned is getting maximum value from its staff.

Different agenda

Life coaching, as we have seen, has the client's agenda as the prime focus. Coaching in the workplace necessarily has the organisation's agenda as paramount. The two agendas may overlap but they are rarely identical. Having said this, there are some organisations enlightened enough to realise that to offer personal and confidential life coaching to their staff would get the desired results even more quickly. Their employees would either gain the awareness and skills to realise their full potential in the company or they would come to the conclusion that their real ambitions lay elsewhere and would leave rather than work half-heartedly.

Different relationship

There is also a difference in the relationship between coach and client. It is often assumed that if coaching is to take place at work, it is the managers who will coach their staff. This means there is an imbalance in the coaching relationship – the expert/learner and senior/junior aspects – which is not present in the equal roles played by life coach and client.

However hard the manager tries to talk 'equally' to an employee, the hierarchy will always be apparent, and true confidentiality is unlikely. The employee cannot choose his manager as a client chooses a life coach. Coaching at work takes place in a particular environment and for a particular reason. The element of choice is missing.

Different skills

The skills of the manager-coach are in many ways similar to those of the life coach but they are used in a more restricted way. Some may not be used at all. While many managers are naturally skilled, or trained to be so, in workplace coaching, there are aspects of the employee's agenda that are 'off-limits'. It is unlikely that the managers will offer new perspectives or provide new vocabulary for their staff. The managers will possibly shy away from discussing with the employees their personal feelings, a wider vision or a deeper spirituality, all acceptable areas in life coaching. It is also likely that the skills of listening, acknowledging and questioning will take second place to advising, requesting and strategising. Many managers in today's pressured work environment will find it difficult to set aside the time to acquire the full range and depth of skills normally associated with life coaching.

Coaching the workforce

The Industrial Society recently published a report – 'New Community or New Slavery?' – which divides employees by their attitudes into 'willing workers' or 'wage slaves'. The former enjoy their work, taking responsibility for their own careers, taking risks and having a more personal, individual relationship with the company that employs them. The latter see work simply as a necessary evil, a means to earn enough money to live and possibly to enjoy themselves outside working hours.

> "It surprises me that so few businesses take Maslow's hierarchy into account when they structure their methods of motivating staff and employees. They resort to traditional methods of motivation as the best or the only ones available....What worked in the past may no longer be appropriate today."
>
> John Whitmore

In an increasing number of organisations, efforts are being made to transform 'wage slaves' into 'willing workers'. The buzz words are staff empowerment, mentoring schemes, flexibility, employee surveys, company shares, and a choice of benefits. The motives are not entirely altruistic because good staff will vote with their feet and organisations want to discourage skilled and expensively trained people from walking out of the door.

So what about mentors? As we saw in Chapter 1, there can be drawbacks to finding and keeping a mentor.

> "Much is said about the need for mentors in career development, but the transient and highly competitive nature of business today does not make a fertile environment for producing them."
>
> John R O'Neil

It may be difficult to find and keep a good mentor; there is no such problem with a life coach. For women especially, there is often the drawback that if they prefer a female mentor, there are fewer available because of the scarcity of senior women in most organisations. This problem doesn't occur with choosing a coach as there is an abundance of excellent women coaches.

When computers can do most of the work, the skills that are most precious are those that only humans can offer – 'people skills'. The provision of coaching in this area for IT professionals is particularly worthwhile. They tend to be analytical, logical and independent, focusing on their own patch and their own results. As they rise up the company hierarchy, as many do, their technical skills grow less important and the quality of their social and personal communication becomes much more significant. Often they are not good at motivating their staff or giving them feedback. Many also struggle with delegation, believing they are the only ones who can do the job properly. Because they tend to concentrate exclusively on the task in hand, they tend to become oblivious of what goes on around them and to miss out almost completely on networking and office politics.

Wise IT professionals use a coach to interact more effectively with clients, both internal and external, and with other team members. The coach can also help them to transform themselves from 'those who do the job' to 'the leaders of those who do the job'. The strategies may include learning to eliminate unnecessary tasks, to prioritise their working days, to delegate and inspire and even to identify and train up their replacement in order to hasten their own promotion. It should be said that, in many companies, the need for coaching in these skills is widespread and not restricted to those in the IT department.

Another area for concern in the workplace is the rise of stress-related illness and absence. The CBI reports that stress-related absence in the UK accounts for the loss of 187 million working days at the cost of £12 billion. The 2000 Survey of Employee Benefits states that the percentage of companies offering help in dealing with stress has risen sharply from only 18% in 1991 to 53% in 1999. It would be charitable to assume that this was due to an increased concern for the welfare of their staff, but it also true that there are heavy financial implications since many workers are suing their employers for unbearable stress and are winning large amounts in compensation. The genuinely concerned companies would do well to consider offering personal coaching as a much less costly way of ensuring their staff were able to deal with the pressures of their work.

Coaching or training?

For many companies, training is seen as an expensive luxury and sometimes they are right. Even the experts are unconvinced. Sir John Whitmore notes that certain managers send their staff "…on a training course or two and kid themselves that that will do it. They seldom get their money's worth." and in *The Empty Raincoat*, Charles Handy comments "Courses can help people to think more clearly, but they cannot change their behaviour or their personalities or most of their values."

The senior manager of a successful business commented, "Companies now hire for attitude not skills. The former cannot be taught, the latter can." Looked at in one way this is right – you cannot teach attitudes. But from a different angle, this is a seriously flawed statement. It exposes the preconceptions of those in authority that everything must be taught. One of the bedrock beliefs of the coach is that attitudes can be examined and changed, but the change takes place through the motivation and wisdom of the client, not the coach.

Training and coaching compared

Training	Coaching
Often off-site: time, travel and venue time expenses	No travelling and only minimal costs
Concentrates on job or specific objectives	Focuses on the whole person
Short time span	Longer time span
Often general and superficial	Deep and lasting
Short term effects – soon tends to lose impact	Long term effects – impact maintained by regular sessions
Not always appropriate to each individual	Always appropriate to each individual
Expert v learner	Equal partnership
Group dynamics – can be distracting	One-to-one – no distractions
Trainer's attention diluted through group	Coach concentrates completely on client
Trainee may feel inadequate when compared with other trainees	Client concentrates on self-comparison
Practical exercises with other trainees – active learning in classroom setting	Tasks set by coach – active learning takes place in real world
Measuring effectiveness – difficult without regular review	Regular review of effectiveness at start of each coaching session
Results in competence	Results in excellence

The point of this comparison is not to demonstrate that training is worthless and coaching is the answer to everything. Clearly the results of coaching do have advantages over those of training but the ideal provision for staff is a combination of the two. The results of a study (published in Public Personnel Management, Winter 1997) showed that where training alone was offered, productivity increased by 22.4% but a combination of training and coaching resulted in a productivity increase of a staggering 88%. In a survey by the IPD in 1999, 800 training managers reported that 87% of organisations are currently using coaching and mentoring. Over 50% believe that this percentage will increase and these newer methods of development are more effective than traditional training courses.

> "To use coaching successfully we have to adopt a far more optimistic
> view than usual of the dormant capability of people, all people."
>
> John Whitmore

Coaching in the workplace need not necessarily be a continuous process. Workers may dip into and out of coaching as they feel the need. The coach may be in regular use when the worker is planning or carrying out a specific project, then possibly used less frequently when working life is relatively plain sailing. The workers may call again if they become demotivated or stressed. Some forward-thinking businesses employ a coach to be retained and used by their staff in this 'on demand' way. Another aspect is the kudos of having a personal coach and in some companies, this option is offered as part of a flexible benefits package. Such a declaration on the importance of individual staff development inspires loyalty and commitment.

> "Offering choice provides other benefits too. It encourages people to
> do things in their own preferred style, technique or sequence within
> the confines of the agreed goal. This allows them to employ and optimise
> their own unique combination of qualities to achieve the best result."
>
> John Whitmore

 A story

Enter first applicant.
  "You understand that this is a simple test we are giving you before we offer you the job you have applied for?"
  "Yes."
  "Well, what is two plus two?"
  "Four."

Enter second applicant.
  "Are you ready for the test?"
  "Yes."
  "Well, what is two plus two?"
  "Whatever the boss says it is."

The second applicant got the job.

Managers as coaches

The role of the manager is undergoing a major rethink and in some cases being eliminated altogether. Managers are now expected to put an end to the 'blame game', to accept their people's feelings as important, to encourage team working, and to use the dreaded word 'empowerment' without batting an eyelid. The idea of manager as coach is not new but is beginning to take on an increased urgency as the expectations of workers increase to include not merely the having of a job, but satisfaction in doing it, and the time for a personal life outside it.

In the past, the main advantage managers had over their staff was their experience. This is now devalued currency. The hectic pace of business change – exemplified starkly by the dot.com revolution – means that no-one has had any relevant experience in the new world of e-business. It's all new and unknown. The most senior of managers may also be those whose past experience is a hindrance rather than a help. Nevertheless, with the demise of many flashy new web-based businesses, there's now a return to the traditional values of actually running a profitable business, making money from serving its customers in a way they are prepared to pay for. So for managers, reading the future is becoming more difficult by the minute. A senior manager commented: "The demand for coaching is being fuelled by the pace of change and the pressure on staff who have been promoted to senior positions much earlier than in previous generations."

In *The Paradox of Success*, John O'Neil makes a comparison between the old and the new in organisational structure. The older companies are hierarchical, use knowledge as power by keeping it in the hands of the few, rewarding those who build a power base and protect it. The workers are informed only of what they 'need to know' and they are not asked for their opinions. They are judged more on how long they spend in the workplace than on how effectively they work. Middle management is still strong and the main thrust is to hold on to strategies that have been successful in the past.

> "..command-and-control organisations are based on the premise that a power and knowledge hierarchy is the most effective way of structuring an organisation. People at the top make the decisions and people further down implement those decisions, changing them as little as possible.."
>
> James Flaherty

By contrast, the new organisations discourage the withholding of information. The systems are structured to keep knowledge and experience flowing freely, wherever and whenever it's needed. Managers are rewarded for empowering others and building effective, flexible teams. Diversity is valued and learning is constantly acquired and quickly put to use. Business ethics, concern for the environment and real valuing of human capital are high on the agenda. A major goal of such companies is to ensure that the people who work for them have job satisfaction and a balanced, integrated life.

> "We used to design organisations to prevent people from making mistakes. We now try to design them to help people make a positive difference."
>
> Charles Handy

Rob

Rob was always juggling activities – constant meetings, international travel and long working days. He felt that he had to do everything himself and that there was no support or recognition for his efforts. As a result he was stressed, feeling undervalued and actively trying to find a job in another company. Rob's confidence seemed extremely low and he was seeing only the worst side of everything. To give him a more balanced view, his coach prompted him to start collating a weekly list of all his achievements. This helped him acknowledge his contributions to work more clearly and by telling his coach about them and jointly celebrating his successes his confidence steadily grew and the list of achievements got longer. Rob's coach then asked him to outline what acceptable working hours and time away from home would be for him. With this in mind he started taking more control of his time and was able to find ways of being more effective and preserving other activities that were important to him. With support he became more assertive in requesting more resources when needed. He also became able to trust other people to take on responsibility from him.

Rob felt that his ability and achievements were not being recognised and had little hope that his next role would give him the opportunity he wanted. Talking this through with his coach, he began to see that lack of active recognition may be due to his manager's style rather than any reflection of his performance. He agreed to ask for feedback and was pleasantly surprised by his manager's views on his abilities and contribution and excited by the possibilities presented for his future development.

Rob is now happy and productive in his current role without it taking a great toll on his life. He is thinking about ' what next' in a very positive way. The next step will probably be with his existing company. If he does decide to move, it will be for the right reasons rather than simply to escape from a problem.

Coaching for managers

Coaching, according to Sir John Whitmore, "is a way of managing, a way of treating people, a way of thinking, a way of being." We have seen that managers wear at least two hats – getting the job done and growing their people. Coaching is one process which achieves both results. Teaching coaching skills to managers is ineffective if they don't have the inner beliefs which would inspire them to use those skills. The best way to learn about coaching is to have a coach.

Managers very often lack training in motivating people and in listening skills. Many would like to do it better but don't know how and don't have time to find out. With a coach, they would experience a very cost- and time-effective way to build these skills. The coach is also a supportive source of advice and a sounding board, usually more readily available than one's immediate superior. Part of the coach's service is to be on call, via phone or email, virtually whenever needed.

Roger

Roger is the owner of six specialised independent communication agencies that he helped put together. He wanted to group them under one banner and get them to work as a unit. The plan was is his mind for months but he did nothing because he was afraid that the individual associates might dislike the project and resist the idea, or walk away if pressure was applied for them to join.

Roger took the decision to employ a coach to help him sort out the issues and get the project off the ground. He gave it a deadline of six months. Through questioning and clarification, his coach helped Roger to clarify his fears and to realise that his project had to be 'bought' by his associates. His first major insight was his need to actually sell them the idea instead of just expecting them to pick it up by osmosis or by reading his mind. Together, Roger and his coach worked on a strategy, deciding how best to market his ideas to his associates to get them on board. Dates were set for individual meetings between Roger and each of his partners.

Roger felt insecure about the whole project because it was new territory and he wasn't in the habit of opening up to other people's points of view or to revealing his weak areas. When he became aware of this, he took steps to improve his communication skills. After the successful integration of the agencies, Roger was able to look back on the whole process and see how his coach helped him to focus on what was important, to be clear about the issues and to gain the skills necessary to complete the project as quickly and effortlessly as possible.

Executive coaching

> "I think boards who go into rhapsodic and romantic overtures about leadership never really define what they mean by that word, nor do they pay enough attention to the human factor."
>
> Warren Bennis

At a meeting of the World Economic Forum held at the beginning of 2001, a seminar was held under the title 'The CEO for the 21st Century: Mission Impossible?' This was a welcome acknowledgement that being a CEO is an increasingly stressful and thankless role. The external daily challenges include:

- Pressure to meet employment targets
- Growing complexity and competitiveness caused by globalisation
- Constant restructuring and management of change
- Increasingly demanding customers
- Problems with recruitment of high quality people
- Keeping abreast of technical innovations
- The demands of environmental pressure groups

The internal daily challenges include:

- Growing and developing emotionally
- Making creative connections in a disconnected world
- Empathising
- Managing stress
- Resisting the ego

Many CEOs feel that everyone expects them to know exactly what to do in any given situation, when often they don't. They have to make quick decisions but still maintain a long-term view. Their plans have to be flexible, ready to change if necessary. Yet those who listen to fresh information and change their views as a result are often characterised as 'weak', with the insult 'U-turn' hurled at them. In a world of constant change, the weakness is not to change with it. Only a fool would persist in a course of action which is clearly heading for disaster simply in order not to be seen to 'U-turn'. But they have to pretend and show no 'weakness' or self-doubt. In other words, they have to be superhuman. Cranfield School of Management research revealed that the UK's top 350 quoted companies, on average, replace their CEO every five years. Senior executives are stressed to such an extent that one in ten has sought medical help.

> "Long-distance leaders recognise the value of an objective, tough-minded critic who is not afraid to point out what others would keep hidden. This may be someone within a company, but sometimes more usefully an outside consultant."
>
> John R O'Neil

For many leaders, this 'critic' is in fact an executive coach. In the safe environment of the coaching session, they can explore what their values and those of their company are and why it's important to the health of an organisation that everyone, particularly the leader himself, knows and works by these values.

> "Executive coaches make an impact on society as a whole because they coach with individuals and teams who have a wide scope of impact on the world."
>
> ICF Conf. 1999

Business coaching

In recent years there has been a big rise in the number of people going freelance or setting up their own business. This is a growth area for coaching as freelancers are notoriously isolated and forgo the support structure that is taken for granted in a job. Self-employment also involves self-promotion – not an easy process and one that requires not only marketing skills but also huge amounts of self-confidence. Coping with such demands is considerably easier with a supportive coach. She can help design the business from scratch and assist the client in planning the transition from employed to self-employed. The confidence to go ahead can also be gained from regular coaching sessions. The client can work out the strengths and weaknesses both of the business idea and his own personality. It is then much easier to manage the weaknesses and build on the strengths.

The coach can be one step ahead and see what is coming next to prepare the client in advance. The would-be entrepreneur need never be caught not knowing where to turn next. This is especially important in the case of cashflow, and of finances generally. Using a coach for this one transition in life is likely to be the best value for money in any business start-up expenses.

Marcus

"I'm the owner of a small garden design business. I set it up straight after leaving horticultural college – it's what I've always dreamed of doing. I've never fancied working for anyone else. Things are 'blooming', if you'll forgive the pun, and now I need to decide how best to grow the business without overreaching myself or giving myself too much stress. I've never been very good with figures but I've got a good accountant. At the moment I employ two people and they're working at full stretch. I've tried talking to professional business advisers – they only have a limited amount of time and they never seem to be quite on the same wavelength as me. What I'd really like is to have regular meetings with someone who would listen to my plans, bounce ideas around with me and who would be as interested as I am in building a great business. Perhaps what I need is a partner?"

After joining his local Chamber of Commerce, Marcus heard about coaching. He decided to find one of his own and his business is now going from strength to strength.

SEVEN

Choosing and using a coach

 A story

> A famous guru gives out a piece of wisdom every day. People gather round to hear his words. Today with a wry smile he says, "All I do is sit by the bank of the river, selling river water."

We all have free access to the water in the river of life. We could all help ourselves to it. But most of us don't. We assume we can't. We gaze longingly at the water but conclude that it would be too difficult, too presumptuous or too selfish to scoop some up for ourselves. Now more and more of us are finding that paying someone to scoop it up for us, until we learn to scoop it up for ourselves, is money well spent. That, in a nutshell, is what we pay a life coach to do.

> "A client has to be willing to bring an outsider into their life. Their whole life, that is."
>
> Thomas J Leonard

Coaching works best for people who:

- recognise that there is a gap between where they are and where they want to be
- can work well with a partner
- are willing to communicate – to talk and to listen and to be open-minded
- are ready to think in new and unfamiliar ways

- are prepared to hear and accept truths which they've so far successfully avoided looking at
- are willing to make substantial changes and take the necessary actions
- accept that the results of coaching are their responsibility, not the coach's.

Coaching is unlikely to work for people who:

- are unwilling to take action or make changes
- only want validation for their own beliefs or simply approval of themselves and what they've achieved
- want complete control over what they do and don't want to listen to suggestions or advice
- are psychologically damaged – possibly in need of therapy or counselling
- suffer from addictive or compulsive behaviour, or who are needy or dependent, desperate for the coach's attention or wanting to be told what to do
- are unable to find the time for regular sessions because of too many other priorities.

Situations when life coaching is particularly worthwhile:

- facing personal or financial challenges
- ready to go for a big opportunity or project
- making big changes, decisions or change of direction
- feeling exhausted, stuck, frustrated or blocked
- needing to enhance skills or increase job satisfaction
- wanting to start or improve your own business
- needing to find a better balance between work and personal life.

Choosing the right coach for you

Because the decisions your coach helps you make may be the most important in your life, finding the right coach is crucial. Be clear in your mind what qualities and background you would prefer your coach to have. There are good coach referral sites on the Net that will help you to shortlist a selection of possible coaches for you. Ask around among your colleagues and friends to see if they recommend a particular coach or coaching service. Ideally, make appointments to talk to at least three coaches.

The trial session

Most coaches will offer a free session with no strings attached. Some coaches refer to this as their 'Living Brochure' because, instead of a printed leaflet describing what they offer, they request that you experience it at first hand. You can use this complimentary call to assess the suitability of the coach for your needs and to ask any questions you may have. The coach may send a brief questionnaire for you to focus on before you go ahead with this session – what's happening in your life and why you're considering using a coach's help.

What you listen for:

- good rapport and compatibility
- attentive listening
- straightforward and constructive questions
- appropriate experience
- respect for your views
- objectivity
- no guarantees, because success depends on the client

What the coach listens for:

- your most pressing issue
- the gaps between where you are now and where you want to be
- what you *don't* say
- the willingness to invest in yourself
- the understanding that you are responsible for the results
- good rapport and compatibility

After the free coaching session you may want to ask some of these questions:

- How long have you been coaching?
- How many clients have you coached?
- What is your professional background and experience?
- Are you professionally trained and accredited? If so, by which organisation?
- How is your coaching service offered – email, telephone, face-to-face?
- What value-added services do you provide for your clients?
- Can I contact any of your current or previous clients?
- Do you have a coach of your own?
- Do you have a coaching specialism or niche?

Ask some questions about the coach's own life. Does she 'walk the talk' or appear to have problems of her own? No-one is perfect, of course, but you should get a clear impression that the coach is under no particular stress and shows no inappropriate emotions when you talk to her. Avoid any coach who sounds desperate to secure you as a client, or one who does not offer to put you in touch with other possible coaches if you so request.

Money matters

Deciding to employ a coach is for many people a major investment in their own future. Ask about the fees but do not be immediately put off if you think they are too high. Talk to the coach and discuss ways in which you could afford it. Some coaches offer a limited number of 'pro bono' places in their practice, or have a system of 'scholarship' places which they offer to clients who cannot afford the fees. Another possibility is for the coaching to focus on financial issues to the point where paying the fees is no longer a problem for you. If you compare the coach's fees with the cost of eating out, gym subscriptions, beauty treatments or holidays, you may well decide that buying the services of a coach is one of the best investments you can make at this particular juncture of your life.

The client pays the coach for the service. The investment is in yourself. If the fees seem expensive for what's on offer, remind yourself of the story about the plumber. The plumber mended the customer's faulty boiler by simply tapping on a single screw and gave him a bill for £100. The customer was aghast and expressed his astonishment –"A hundred pounds just for tapping a screw!" The plumber replied, "No, £1 for tapping the screw. £99 pounds for knowing exactly which screw to tap and how hard to tap it." It's a good parallel for the coaching service. Client: "£250 just for one and half hours of your time a month!" Coach: "No, £50 for the time – £200 for knowing exactly what questions to ask, when and how to ask them, and how to listen to the answers."

The people who use life coaches aren't fools – quite the opposite – and they would not continue to pay the fees if they didn't believe they were getting value for money. Research quoted in The Orlando Sentinel (18 July 1999) showed that of 210 coaching clients interviewed, 98.5% reckoned their investment was well worth the money spent. It is the client's responsibility to ensure that they get value for money.

As in the early days of any profession, there are those who jump on the band wagon, call themselves coaches but who do not bother with the tiresome business of actually undergoing any training. At the time of writing, the position is that anyone can claim to be a coach, so you need to be certain that you are not paying for a second-rate service. The proof of the pudding is in the eating. If, during the free trial session, anything gives you cause for concern, be honest about it to the coach. This is a time to listen carefully to your gut feelings and act on them. Ask yourself "Would I look forward to regular sessions with this coach?"

Making the decision

If you want a coach initially for help with a particular aspect of your life, or for a well-defined project, you may want to consider one of the many specialist coaches. There are coaches who offer skills and experience in different niches. Weight loss, stopping smoking, starting a business, writing a book, improving relationships – the list is endless. You will almost certainly find what you are looking for on the coach referral websites.

If your main issue is job-related, it is not necessary for your coach to have experience in your area of work. Sometimes it's better if she doesn't. She will be able to see things with fresh eyes and ask questions that people from within the industry may not think to ask. In some circumstances it is important for your coach to be familiar with the type of issues you are facing, but she should still be able to stand back and see the bigger picture.

When you are happy that you have found the right coach for you, you will probably be asked to sign up for a minimum length of time. Some coaches will ask for at least a three-month commitment; others will ask for six months or even a year, depending upon how they run their coaching service. The reason for this is that it can take some time for clients to become aware of what needs to be changed and to see a real difference in their lives. A deep and lasting transformation is not likely to be effected via a 'quick fix'.

> "Cultivating mindfulness may require some changes in your usual modes of thought. You may have to listen instead of talking, be thoughtful rather than reactive, put off decisions rather than displaying your ability to make them on the spur of the moment."
>
> John R O'Neil

Some clients experience a 'three month plateau' when the initial excitement and expectancy of being coached has worn off because the client realises exactly how much remains to be done, how the changes he is making are not necessarily comfortable for himself or others in his life, and that once he has taken up the challenge of living his life to its full potential, there's no turning back. Ironically, the truth is that the 'plateau' is actually the place where the greatest amount of learning takes place. Staying with your coach is essential, to keep you on track, maybe even raising the stakes. You may find your coach ratcheting things up a gear so that your expectations of what you can achieve are also raised.

Different coaches will have different degrees of flexibility which allow a client, after the initial commitment period, to cut down the number of sessions per month, or even to reduce to a single 'top-up' call once a month. It is important to check this out at the beginning of your coaching partnership. It is unlikely that you will find any coach completely inflexible and most will allow you to discontinue the relationship at any time after an agreed period of notice. There is clearly no advantage for coaching to continue when the client is unwilling for it to do so.

Making a start

Your coach may start with goal-setting (the future), or with eliminating anything that is slowing you down or draining your energy (the present).

Your coach will be careful not to allow you to concentrate on the future as a way of escaping an unsatisfactory present. Only when the client accepts the present as 'perfect' can meaningful goals be set. A good coach will ask you about your values and needs before she asks about your goals. It's vital to discover who you are before you can think clearly about who you want to become or what you want to do. You will be asked to concentrate on making life easier and attracting what you want rather than making hard work of it and struggling.

The practicalities

The coaching process will involve a number of regular sessions, usually 30–40 minutes, once a week or three a month. Also, your coach may offer short phone calls between sessions, and unlimited emails. Some coaches run a 'Coaching Gym' along the lines of a keep-fit gym where you pay a monthly or yearly subscription and use the equipment any time you want, the 'equipment' in this case being the coach.

Some coaches offer face-to-face sessions and this would normally incur the expenses of time and travel. 'Telecoaching' can take place almost anywhere and at any time. Some clients initially have doubts about the effectiveness of being coached over the phone and of course there are advantages and disadvantages but the former far outweigh the latter. The cons are the perceived problems of not being able to read each other's body language and not having any of the usual visual 'clues'. You may also want to see exactly who you're dealing with. On the other hand, not having such clues means there are no instant judgements on either side. Talking on the phone allows you (and your coach!) to conceal your facial expressions. You are likely to listen more intently and be more willing to tell the truth to someone whom you can't see and are unlikely ever to meet. Telecoaching eliminates all the hassle of travel, there are no safety issues and, with the ubiquitous mobile phone, no geographical limits. Some coaches offer group coaching over the telephone and, if you are happy to share sessions with others, this can be a more affordable option.

Email is also a powerful coaching tool – more cost-effective than face-to-face meetings or long-distance telephone calls. If the coach and client are in different countries, there is no problem of time zones. The response time is flexible. It can be immediate so that there is in effect a conversation taking place, or with a time lag, allowing space for reflection and research. People are more willing to be direct and honest when there is a space of some kind between themselves and the respondent. Research into email coaching reveals that women benefit from it more than men because it cuts out many of the barriers of a male-dominated workplace. Women are also more likely to have the speedy keyboard skills necessary to make email coaching quick and effective.

There are a number of websites that now offer coaching as live on-line coaching. This is offered for individuals and groups and can be an interesting way of sharing a coaching session with other people. Often, there is a set theme to the coaching, with the coach facilitating a discussion amongst the group. At the time of writing, it is probably fair to say that this idea has not yet fully caught on, but with more and more people going on-line for support with personal development issues, online coaching has real potential as another accessible way to work on a particular issue with a coach.

The coaching sessions

Your coach will encourage you to talk about:

- What you've achieved
- Problems you've faced and how you handled them
- What you're currently working on
- New awareness and insights
- What you need from the session
- What your major learning point is from this session
- What you want most from the next session.

If it's true that everyone has the answers to their own problems, why use a coach at all? Because you'll find those answers, and live them, much more quickly with the support of a good coach. The coach's role is not to make decisions for you but to widen your range of options. Once you get used to being coached, you'll find it's an indispensable tool and wonder how you managed so long without it. You may also find that from time to time, you may need to change your coach. Different coaches have different strengths and you may outgrow what your current coach has to offer. Any well-trained coach will accept this or even positively encourage it.

Coaching is a bit like scaffolding. It provides support, structure and safety while a building is under construction. Once the building is finished, the scaffolding is put away until it's needed again, possibly for a higher, more ambitious construction. A coach offers a framework for the client until his goals are achieved or until he feels able to progress on his own.

> The Props assist the House
> Until the House is built
> And then the Props withdraw
> And adequate, erect,
> The House supports itself
> And cease to recollect
> The Auger and the Carpenter –
> Just such a retrospect
> Hath the perfected Life –
> A past of Plank and Nail
> And slowness – then the Scaffolds drop
> Affirming it a Soul.
>
> Emily Dickinson

EIGHT

Life coaching and the future

"Travellers, there is no path. Paths are made by walking."

Antonio Machado

For life coaching as a profession, the future looks good. It is already flourishing in the States with around 10,000 coaches offering a wide spectrum of specialisms. Though less well known in Europe, it is nevertheless catching up quickly. In May, 2001, the 1st International Coaching Federation (ICF) Conference took place in Grindelwald, Switzerland, attracting over 350 coaches from 22 countries. They gathered for the first time in Europe to share ideas, speakers, workshops and resources. The conference demonstrated just how speedily the profession of coaching generally is expanding. Many different disciplines were represented – corporate, executive, business, holistic – proving that every one-to-one coaching relationship is in essence a form of life coaching.

The ICF was set up to build, support and preserve the integrity of the coaching profession and to consolidate a foundation of proactive self-regulation. It is vital that the clients, who are partners in the success of the profession, feel confident to recommend life coaching to even the most sceptical and cynical of enquirers. Professional credibility is essential because the public is being educated, chiefly by the media, in the importance of scrutinising a potential coach's qualifications. On the other hand, there is some resistance among coaches to too much regulation because as a profession, it is an art rather than a science – or perhaps, at its best, a blend of both. It is above all a creative and intuitive business and we must beware of crushing it beneath too much legislation.

If we lift our eyes from the practicalities of the profession, there is an exciting picture for the future. If the purpose of life coaching is empowering people to be who they really are, then a whole new vision for the human race becomes possible.

A new kind of leader

Our leaders today are traditionally the elite people 'at the top' who have the majority 'below' them looking to them for inspiration and guidance. They are executive directors of organisations, senior bureaucrats, government leaders, presidents and prime ministers. They are usually drawn from small, select groups who have special access to money, power and education. In the past they have had clear ideas of why they are there and what is expected of them. But now these people need to change. An interesting indication of this is the huge increase in books for the power holders encouraging them to explore and develop their 'spiritual capital'. Such titles as 'Leadership and Spirit', 'Spirited Leading and Learning' and 'Leading without Power' are suddenly springing up and multiplying. Such material would have been unthinkable only a couple of decades ago. Even the definition of a leader has fundamentally changed.

> "The leader of the past was a person who knew how to tell. The leader of the future will be a person who knows how to ask."
>
> Peter Drucker

These new leaders may be anyone, anywhere, from the self-empowerment guru Anthony Robbins to the businesswoman Anita Roddick; from the heroine of the high seas, Ellen McArthur, to the dedicated human rights activist, James Mawdsley. They are exemplars of this truth:

> "Leadership is not simply something we do. It comes from somewhere inside us. Leadership is a process, an intimate expression of who we are."
>
> Kevin Cashman

According to Charles Handy in *The Empty Raincoat*, Tony Benn, the British socialist politician, said: 'There are kings and prophets. The kings have the power and the prophets have the principles.' Handy continues:

> "I am on the side of the kings, the people who make things happen, but every king needs his prophet, to help him, and increasingly her,

to keep a clear head amidst confusions. No one, however, would want the prophet to run the show.

Prophets, in spite of their name, do not foretell the future . . . What prophets do is to tell the truth as they see it. They can point to the emperor's lack of clothes, that things are not what people like to think they are. They can warn of dangers ahead if the course is not changed. They can, and often did, point their fingers at what they thought to be wrong, unjust or prejudiced. Most of all they can offer a way of thinking about things, a way to clarify the dilemmas and concentrate the mind.

What the prophet cannot, and should not, do is to tell the doers what to do . . . The prophet can provide a chart but cannot dictate where or how the vessel should sail."

If for the word 'prophet' we substitute 'coach', the passage is an exact description of the relationship between leaders and their coaches. It's not about coaches knowing all the answers, but knowing how to ask the right questions, how to challenge the leader's assumptions, to discover their true values and to develop the skills needed to be a great leader. The coach may be the only person who focuses the leader on him or herself as a person, and what their own needs and values are and to live by them.

Two vital aspects of the new leadership are that it is a journey, not a destination, and that it is chiefly about being, not doing. One development in the area of leadership is the rise of women as leaders.

"Women know, with a confidence that they have not had before, that they are as good as men – as clever, as competent, as capable – and that there are new ways of doing almost anything."

Harriet Harman

In *The Paradox of Success*, John R O'Neil notes that long-distance leaders of the future are likely to be persons who:

- are comfortable in multiple roles – learner, teacher, team player
- are not strictly defined by their education or work status
- are flexible and non-hierarchical
- are accustomed to self-analysis and in tune with their feelings
- are willing to seek support
- are determined to have a life outside of work.

O'Neil adds "This description already applies to many of today's women leaders, who embody many qualities of long-distance leadership better than men." Women are becoming more acceptable as leaders because of the perception of authority shifting from doing to being, with a greater acceptance of the power of intuition, traditionally seen as a female strength.

A new kind of people

"Do not wait for leaders. Do it alone, person to person."

Mother Teresa

Instead of waiting for their leaders to catch up with what's needed in the twenty-first century, many people are going on ahead to achieve what they want without leadership. They are exploring deeper aspects of life, many of which were in the recent past thought too embarrassing to talk about. There are books, websites, workshops, festivals, all devoted to the widening spiritual awareness of which life coaching is an integral part. It is another version of the 'fish symbol':

> "The early Christians used the fish symbol as a way of testing the response of another person to see if it was safe to keep on talking. They would draw a little fish symbol in the sand and if the other person responded appropriately they would say, 'Alright, here's a brother so we can talk honestly'. I think people are using words like consciousness, creativity and intuition in very much the same way."

Willis Harman

Charles Handy believes "we really have to unlearn the way we dealt with the past in order to deal with the future." He is talking about businesses and organisations but the statement is equally true for individuals. It is what coaches do with their clients. They help them to see how they, as human beings, have been programmed and conditioned to fit into what will soon be 'the past' and how they can learn new ways of living their lives, creating their own future, not fitting into a preordained one. As Handy reminds us"

"A decent society has, annoyingly perhaps, to start with us, with each one of us, and with what we, individually, believe we could be, and what we believe a decent society ought to look like."

A new kind of freedom

Until we are free
to think for ourselves
our dreams are not free
to unfold.

Nancy Kline

Possibly the most important service a life coach provides for a client is to be a guide towards personal freedom. Such freedom consists of freedom *from*:

- being a victim of circumstances
- the chatter of gremlins
- the expectations of society
- external authority
- fear of failure
- slavery to the desire for money and status

And freedom *to*:

- discover and develop your authentic self
- choose your own destiny
- choose your own friends and community
- show your emotions
- choose your own responses to events and people
- seek out the true purpose of your life.

"...one of the most fundamental challenges of our times: the willingness for an individual, an organisation, a community, a country, ultimately the entire human species, to take responsibility for what it has created and not blame anyone...To put ourselves on the line – with passion, with conviction, with gusto and with boldness of imagination"

David Gershon

A vision for life coaching

With the move into the 21st century, we are on the edge of great opportunities to change for the better, with a plethora of challenging and exhilarating ideas around and a distinct feeling that evolution has not ended for the human race.

When we read or hear about the seismic changes occurring in the world today – the technological revolution, information overload, population shifts, economic globalisation – these are presented as external, objective happenings. Much less is said about the internal changes taking place in the hearts and minds of the people living through these times of upheaval, their personal growth and development, their beliefs and spirituality. On the contrary, when that side of the coin is mentioned, it is most often to point the finger of fun at the self-help culture or to denigrate the 'New Age' ethos. This reaction is not without reason as much of the material put out is 'faddy' and nonsensical, focusing on the 'quick fix' which is simply not realistic or possible. But that doesn't mean there isn't a deep and wholesome shift in the way in which we interpret our own existence.

> "As we pass through life, hidden sides of our character continue to emerge and unfold, hungry for new nourishment."
>
> John R O'Neil

The driving impulse of life coaching is that it helps us to discover and feed these 'hidden sides'. Both coach and client seek for 'new nourishment' together. As our internal selves are fed and thrive, so we expand the capabilities and confidence of the human race to deal with the external problems.

People who find the courage to begin their journey of self-discovery are as much pioneers as those who explore jungles or trek across snowy wastes. They too are discovering new worlds and what it means to be human. The true potential of human beings is revealing itself as more amazing by the minute.

It is entirely possible that life coaching will be one of the most important and influential means of changing society and shifting people into a new way of thinking and being. The possibility is there. The only vital ingredients are the excellence of the coaches themselves and the quality of the clients they coach.

In the first chapter, we looked at how coaching differs from mental health services like therapy or counselling. This difference must become clearer and more defined if life coaching is to fulfil the expectations placed upon it. At this crucial point in its development, it must offer something distinctive from the other disciplines, transcending the current methods of personal development and offering an individually tailored service from which anyone can benefit. It encompasses a vision of the world where everyone is encouraged to discover their strengths, to take delight in the world about them and to fulfil their potential. Life coaching, in the hands of skilled and enlightened people, can be the catalyst for people seeing the world and their place in it with new and excited eyes. For some, it will be a long, slow process; for others it comes as a breathtaking flash of insight – the Ah ha! moment.

A visionary, according to Thomas J Leonard, is a person "who has orientated his or her life around expanding, articulating and becoming what they see as possible". It is extraordinarily difficult to do the articulating coherently and on one's own.

George Leonard states that: "Every viable culture and every successful individual needs at least two guardian angels – vision and practice." With a coach, you get these two guardian angels for the price of one!

The coaching fraternity would join with Marilyn Ferguson in declaring: "I'm placing my hope in those people who are awake and who have the courage and conviction to see how many other people they can wake up."

The spread of coaching will depend only minimally on coaches themselves. Mostly it will depend on those who have been coached, who have learned what it feels like and what it achieves, and spread the word to others – by coaching them.

"We have to start really looking into our hearts and seeing what we truly believe to be possible. That's literally what it means to have a vision-led process. The source of the energy comes from your deep belief that something is possible. And it might be something that has never, ever been produced on a large scale, so all your historical evidence says 'no, no, no' – but your heart says 'yes'."

Peter Senge

Life coaching is the best way I know to enable people to listen to their hearts and to act on the 'yes'.

Further reading

Anderson, Nancy. *Work with Passion.* Carroll & Graf Publishers 1984.

Bolles, Richard. *The Three Boxes of Life.* Ten Speed Press 1978.

Bridges, William. *JobShift.* Addison-Wesley Publishing 1994.

Carson, Richard D. *Taming Your Gremlin.* HarperPerennial 1986.

Cashman, Kevin. *Leadership from the Inside Out.* Executive Excellence Publishing 2000.

Covey, Stephen. *The Seven Habits of Highly Effective People.* Simon & Schuster 1992.

de Mello, Anthony. *Awareness.* Doubleday, New York 1990

————. *The Song of the Bird.* Image Books 1984.

DiCarlo, Russell E, ed. *Towards a New World View.* Epic Publishing 1996. (Includes interviews with Marilyn Ferguson, Willis Harman, George Leonard, David Gershon, Gary Zukav, Peter Senge, Stephen Covey, Richard Tarnas and Joan Borysenko)

Downey, Myles. *Effective Coaching.* Orion Business Books 1999.

Dreher, Diane. *The Tao of Personal Leadership.* Thorsons 1997.

Flaherty, James. *Evoking Excellence in Others.* Butterworth-Heinemann 1999.

Fortgang, Laura Berman. *Take Yourself to the Top.* Warner Books Inc 1998.

————. *Living Your Best Life.* HarperCollins 2001.

Fromm, Erich. *Escape from Freedom.* Holt, Reinhart & Winston 1941.

————. *To Have or To Be?* Jonathan Cape Ltd 1978.

Gallwey, Timothy. *The Inner Game of Work.* Orion Business Books 2000.

Gibson, Rowan Ed. *Rethinking the Future.* Nicholas Brealey Publishing Ltd 1996. (Includes interviews with Charles Handy, Warren Bennis and Peter Senge)

Goleman, Daniel. *Emotional Intelligence.* Bloomsbury Publishing plc 1996.

Handy, Charles. *The Empty Raincoat.* Hutchinson 1993.

————. *The Hungry Spirit.* Hutchinson 1997.

Harman, Harriet. *The Century Gap.* Vermilion 1993.

Hill, Dave. *The Future of Men.* Phoenix 1997

Jaworski, Joseph. *Synchronicity – the Inner Path of Leadership.* Berrett-Koehler Publishers Inc 1996.

Kline, Nancy. *Time to Think.* Ward Lock 1999.

Leonard, Thomas J. *The Portable Coach.* Scribner 1998.

O'Neil, John R. *The Paradox of Success.* McGraw-Hill International (UK) Ltd 1995.

Steere, Douglas V. Gleanings: *A Random Harvest.* Abingdon Press 1986

Whitmore, John. *Coaching for Performance.* Nicholas Brealey Publishing Ltd 1992.

————. *Need, Greed or Freedom.* Element Books Ltd 1997.

Whitmyer, Claude, Ed. *Mindfulness and Meaningful Work.* Parallax Press 1994. (Includes essays by Sam Keen, Rick Fields, Ellen Langer and Robert Aitken)

Whitworth, Laura, Henry Kimsey-House and Phil Sandahl. *Co-Active Coaching.* Davies-Black Publishing 1998

The next step

Your starting point for finding a life coach is either to contact any of the coaches listed below or to visit the ICF website and search the Coach Referral Service.

Aboodi Shaby: +44 (0) 1225 862005   coach@aboodi.net
Bill Ford: +44 (0)20 8286 4772   greatcoach@clara.co.uk
Christian Worth: +44 (0) 1342 312835   coach@less-stress-more-success.com

Christina Toft: +44 (0) 1895 420286   Crpimage@aol.com
Christine Baines: +44 (0)1606 350468   ChristineBaines@compuserve.com
Dianna Keel: +44 (0)20 8780 9240   Dianna@coach.tc
Dominique Charles: +44 (0)208 670 6940   dominique@selfdevelopmentcoach.com
Elizabeth Rowlands: 0845 130 8282   TheCoach@placeofpower.com
Gina Harris: +44 (0)1335 350540   enquiries@accesscoaching.co.uk
Ginny Baillie: +44 (0)20 8838 0560   ginny@bandf.org

Janice Morris: +44 (0)191 2843606   jan.morris@cableinet.co.uk
Jilly Shaul: +44 (0)20 8275 0072   lifematters@btinternet.com
Mark Forster: +44 (0) 1403 250016   MarkF1000@aol.com
Mike Duckett: +44 (0) 1494 473504   coach@coachingforsuccess.co.uk
Rachel Spooncer: +44 (0)1928 740779   rachel_spooncer@lineone.net
Resli Costabell: +44 (0)207 7231 0158   ResliCostabel@compuserve.com
Sarah Litvinoff: +44 (0)20 7609 6738   sarahl@dircon.co.uk
Suzanne Looms: +44 (0)20 8651 5898   heart@macline.co.uk

Teresa Marshall: +44 (0)1202 631 127   t.marshall@talk21.com

The International Coaching Federation is the professional association for coaches worldwide. One of the key functions of ICF is also to provide independent credentialling for coaches, thereby helping to uphold the standards and ethics of the profession. There is a coach referral service on the ICF website:

www.coachfederation.org

ICF in the UK:
UK-ICF
PO Box No. 11853
London SW15 5ZF
www.coachfederation.org
info@coachfederation.org

ICF in the USA:
International Coach Federation
1444 1 Street, NW, Suite 700
Washington, DC 20005-6542
ICFOffice@coachfederation.org